"Each time I spoke with Eddie, he would share these fun and insightful tidbits about consumers. They were all surprising—and surgical in their precision and power. Later, I realized his wisdom came from superconsumers. This book is not only chock full of epiphanies; it is also a guide that will help you discover your own superconsumers and benefit from them as I have."

—**DWIGHT BROWN,** Senior Vice President, Marketing, iRobot

"Eddie Yoon taps into a major secret in brand building: every powerful brand derives its strength from an even deeper and more powerful force—the emotion and energy of superconsumers. These tremendously insightful and influential consumers will pay more, explore more, and advocate more. This book helps you understand how to identify them, completely change the way you think about your business, and maximize your growth."

—**MICHELLE STACY,** former President, Keurig Inc.

SUPERCONSUMERS

eddie yoon

SUPERCONSUMERS

A SIMPLE, SPEEDY, AND SUSTAINABLE PATH TO SUPERIOR GROWTH

Harvard Business Review Press

Boston, Massachusetts

Library of Congress Cataloging-in-Publication Data

Names: Yoon, Eddie, author.
Title: Superconsumers : a simple, speedy, and sustainable path to superior
    growth / Eddie Yoon.
Description: Boston, Massachusetts : Harvard Business Review Press, [2016] |
    Includes bibliographical references and index.
Identifiers: LCCN 2016028014 | ISBN 9781633692077 (hardcover)
Subjects: LCSH: Market segmentation. | Consumer behavior. | Consumer
    profiling. | Consumers—Attitudes. | Fans (Persons)—Attitudes.
Classification: LCC HF5415.127 .Y66 2016 | DDC 658.8/343—dc23
LC record available at https://lccn.loc.gov/2016028014

contents

Contents

part one

AN INTRODUCTION TO SUPERCONSUMERS

chapter 1

MAKING YOUR BEST CUSTOMERS BETTER

"Eddie, how do you think we should change the POG?" asked my client, Jeff Ackerberg, the vice president of sales and marketing of a major office-supply manufacturer. POG? I had no idea what he was talking about. The only thing that came to mind was passion-orange-guava juice from Hawaii, where I grew up. "We have a few different versions of the planogram for different retailers, but maybe you have a new idea?" Jeff continued.

The good news was that I figured out that POG was shorthand for planogram, but the bad news was that I still had no idea what a planogram was. Since I was a young consultant, just a few years out of college, I had never before helped a client with retail activation, so I wasn't up to speed with the lingo. But after a long and uncomfortable pause, it hit me: a planogram probably referred to a diagram of a product display.

As my young career was flashing before my eyes, I fell back on the hundreds of hours I had spent listening to consumers of office supplies and the months I had spent analyzing data about what made these people tick. From my research, I knew that while the vast majority of office-supply consumers had zero emotional connection to paper clips, pens, and Post-It notes, one-third of these consumers were fanatics. I'm not kidding. There are people who love office supplies the same way some of us love bacon or our local sports teams.

A woman's face popped into my head. Her name was Sally (not her real name), and she was one of the consumers whom my colleagues and I spoke with when we were researching the office-supply industry. A manager of a car rental agency, she rented hundreds of cars, vans, and trucks to long lines of customers each day. Often she felt set up to fail. She had to keep every promise made to a consumer with a reservation, but consumers could reserve and cancel without penalty or return their rental car earlier or later than their reservation mandated. Reconciling this uncertainty was difficult. And even when she was successful, she was left with a lot of paperwork to process, and the workload could get overwhelming.

Because of the frenetic nature of her job, Sally focused on things she could control. Specifically, she prided herself on her efficiency and organization. When she wasn't dealing with a customer, she would make copies of the rental agreements, punch holes in the contracts, and organize them in a three-ring binder. She took this part of her job very seriously and appreciated any office supplies that were reliable and easy to use. Paperwork might seem like a chore to most people. But to Sally, a three-ring binder full of perfectly organized contracts was like a trophy for a job well done and her way of bringing order to chaos.

Through trial and error, she had settled on the best supplies for her job. The only exception was her hole puncher. Since it was a single-hole kind, she had to manually punch three holes in every page of over a hundred contracts per day. The repetitive task was a lot of work, and her hands would often cramp. But company bureaucracy made it a hassle to get a top-of-the-line three-hole puncher or an electric hole puncher.

Sally's relationship with office supplies, however odd it seemed to me at first, was as rational as chefs' love for their knives. When my colleagues and I gave her a heavy-duty, three-hole puncher as a thank you gift for speaking with us, she covered her mouth and was clearly touched. She told us afterward that this simple and inexpensive gift made her feel deeply understood and respected.

And Sally wasn't alone. From our interviews and data crunching, we discovered that there were five million more consumers, just like Sally, who were passionate about office supplies. And this segment of consumers made up one-third of all consumers in the market in any given year. And better yet, they drove 70 percent of the profit.

Given those facts, we decided to pitch a novel idea: tailor the product display to Sally and her cohort of die-hards. At the time, most office-supply stores placed cheaper, private-label products in their prime shelf space. Since stores didn't think that consumers cared much about office supplies, they put the products with the lowest prices at eye level on the shelf. We went in the opposite direction. I suggested we move the heavy-duty and electric staplers and punchers from the bottom shelf to the eye-level one.

When we took our ideas to three major office-supply retailers, two retailers were impressed—they had never seen this depth of consumer insight in office supplies before and were willing to go along with the reset. In our planogram, we added signage that called out the high-performance staplers and punchers and praised the benefits of jam-free performance. We included electrical outlets so that customers could plug in the products to try them out.

We talked to other functional leaders about the two receptive retailers. We modeled the financial risk and upside with finance, discussed the inventory implications with the supply-chain people, and wrote retailer presentations for sales. Both retailers had doubts but conceded that even if we were partly right and sold even a few more higher-priced and higher-margin items, the return would more than offset any inventory and operational risk. We discussed with marketing if a big advertising campaign was necessary to push these high-end products. We decided against it, because we realized that Sally and those like her shopped or browsed these stores frequently—often, four times per month. Most other consumers shop these stores four times a year, if that. So there was no need for big marketing dollars to drive office-supply die-hards like Sally to the store, as they were already there. They needed to be romanced at retail. They needed to feel the heft of the heavy-duty stapler. They needed to hear the satisfying sound of the electric stapler. They needed to imagine a world without jammed staplers.

The retailers were pleased with the results. In nine months, heavy-duty and electric product sales doubled, and the total category went up 19 percent year after year. The third retailer, which had balked at our idea because we would be displacing its private-label products, saw its sales decline by 9 percent in the same period.

I often reflect back on that meeting with wonder and appreciation. I'm sure that the vice president of sales and marketing knew I was somewhat in over my head, but to his credit, he realized the same thing that I did—that consumers like Sally can be an extraordinarily powerful north star.

This is the essence of what I call a *superconsumer strategy*: find, listen to, and engage with your most passionate customers; understand their tastes, emotions, and behaviors; lean into the aspects that also resonate with a much larger group of potential superconsumers; and then tailor your decision making, coordinate and concentrate your cross-functional investments, and innovate—both your product and your business model—to give these consumers what they want and need. The strategy may seem obvious now, but in my experience of helping companies with their growth strategies, I've seen few managers take this approach to its fullest extent.

I've found that managers who fully embrace a superconsumer strategy, such as the office-supply manufacturer in the story above, learn more from their consumers through increased empathy. These managers are more persuasive at getting buy-in from the leaders in their organization, make better strategic decisions, and achieve more stable, more predictable, and longer-term growth.

MEET THE SUPERCONSUMERS

Any business can profitably grow. This may seem like a silly thing to believe when you look at the tombstones of businesses such as Circuit City and Motorola, the latter of which had the hottest mobile phone on the market just over a decade ago, but my faith comes from superconsumers like Sally.

Unlike *heavy users* (i.e., a product's highest-volume buyers who are defined simply by the quantity of their purchases), superconsumers are characterized by their attitude as well: they are passionate about and highly engaged with—and maybe even a little obsessive about—a category (say, golf equipment, in the case of my dad). They are the sneaker-heads who own dozens of pairs of sneakers. They are the sports fans who own replica jerseys and hang signed memorabilia in their finished basements. They are bacon, chops, and carnitas-loving consumers who call themselves "pork dorks."

Superconsumers aren't random oddballs who buy in bulk. They're emotional buyers who base their purchase decisions on their life aspirations. A superconsumer of Gatorade, for example, doesn't just buy its products because he loves how they taste; he chooses the brand because it represents hard work, and Gatorade's drinks, chews, and protein bars allow him to recover quicker during marathon training. He's "hiring" Gatorade for a job, to help him improve his performance—an allegiance that also ties into a broader life quest, to train for a marathon. He's deeply invested. He wants to "be like Mike." The secret is realizing that for superconsumers, every category has "Gatorade-level" aspirations that can be tapped into.

The same goes for other superconsumers as well. A superconsumer of American Girl dolls sees the products as a way to connect with her grandchildren and spend more time with her family, and a private-label superconsumer sees value-priced groceries as a way to save money for a house while still feeding his family high-quality food.

Superconsumers can be an eclectic bunch who are hard to pin down. But thanks to our parent company, Nielsen, my colleagues and I at the Cambridge Group have access to an enormous amount of data about what people watch and buy. Specifically, we have mined Nielsen's US Homescan database, which consists of approximately one hundred thousand US households that have agreed to have all of their purchases measured across all channels (down to the UPC level). With this information, we created a data set of over 125 consumer-goods categories that represented more than $400 billion in sales. We analyzed the purchase behavior of consumers across demographics and interviewed selected participants about the depth of their feelings about a particular category and why they valued it so much. Thanks to Jeff Eastman, the leader of the Homescan business at Nielsen, we have hundreds of statements from the households about the benefits sought, the emotions felt, and the aspirations held for all these categories.

Because of Nielsen's data set (which is unique in its combination of emotion and economics), we've become superconsumer whisperers, in a sense. We know what makes these people tick and what makes them so beneficial to businesses of all kinds—not just office-supply manufacturers and consumer-goods companies.

The biggest benefit of superconsumers comes down to simple math. Although superconsumers are few in number—usually about 10 percent of consumers for a particular product or category—they can drive between 30 percent and 70 percent of sales, an even greater share of category profit, and usually close to 100 percent of the insights (figure 1-1).

FIGURE 1-1

Superconsumers: the top 10 percent (across 124 consumer packaged goods categories with at least $400 billion in sales)

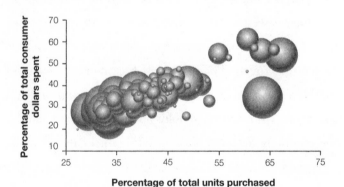

Percentage of total units purchased

Source: Nielsen.

And they aren't particularly price-sensitive. Since they have emotional and aspirational connections to the products they love, they're willing to pay a premium for them as long as those products offer additional benefits that are appealing.

Common sense might suggest that there would be little return on investment (ROI) in trying to sell an office-supply superconsumer who owns eight staplers a ninth or a tenth one. But our analysis proves that selling those additional staplers to superconsumers is a smarter growth strategy than simply selling replacements for broken or lost staplers to normal consumers, because superconsumers buy more products at higher prices. But more important, these consumers are also gurus who can help you innovate and can act as pied pipers who spread the word to other consumers.

As companies build up their analytic capabilities, they are becoming increasingly adept at identifying and engaging superconsumers. When they do, they not only find that these shoppers have good reasons for buying so much, but also often discover a hidden appetite to buy more— even in the most unlikely product categories.

Superconsumers are also more predictable than other consumers since the root cause of their behaviors is deep emotions and motivations rather than socioeconomics (e.g., "they buy because they have high incomes") or demographics (e.g., "they buy because they are young"). Motivations are great because they are wildly variable across consumers (figure 1-2).

There are some motivations people largely agree on (the left side of figure 1-2 represents people who, on a six-point agreement scale, range from agreeing "completely" with a motivation to agreeing "somewhat" with it). Things

FIGURE 1-2

Emotional variance across attitudes: percentage who agree versus percentage who disagree

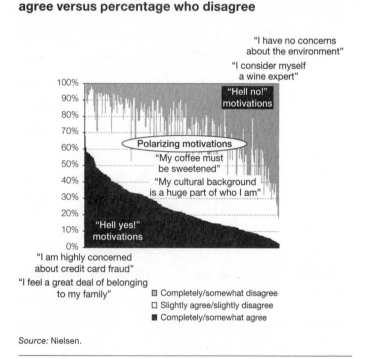

Source: Nielsen.

like fear of credit card fraud or the importance of family are good examples of these "Hell yes!" statements, with which most people agree. Similarly, there are "Hell no!" statements, which range from things like thinking of oneself as a wine expert or a willingness to damage the environment. For these motivations, people are also united in their disagreement. But most of the motivations are in fact polarizing, ranging from the more casual, like how you take your coffee, to the very personal and meaningful, like how important your culture is to your identity.

Polarized feelings lead to distinct behaviors—the ability to target and focus. Focus drives higher ROI and better growth.

Over the decades of our growth-strategy work, we have curated key motivations that drive consumer behavior across thousands of categories. We are systematically integrating these motivations into the Nielsen Homescan panel, which daily collects tens of millions of data points about what people are buying from all types of retailers. This data set, which blends motivational and behavioral data, is unique. Most big data sets are either purely motivational or emotional, with no behavioral link, or vice versa.

Here is an example using the Nielsen US Homescan data set, which shows that emotions were a stronger predictor of higher sales than were demographics (like age and household size) or socioeconomic measures (like income). Thanks to my Cambridge Group colleagues Claire Zhou, Dimitar Antov, and Linda Deeken, we found that emotional engagement made the difference (figure 1-3).

In general, consumers who are more engaged spend appreciably more money on the category than do less engaged consumers. Because this association was intuitive, Zhou, Antov, and Deeken dug deeper with a more rigorous statistical analysis of beer drinkers. They found that consumer motivations account for nearly three-fourths of all beer spending (figure 1-4).

FIGURE 1-3

Annual category spending per household

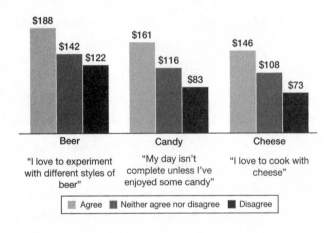

Source: Nielsen.

FIGURE 1-4

Drivers of beer spending

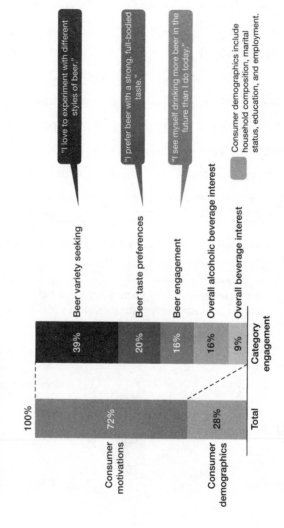

Consumer motivations — 72%

Consumer demographics — 28%

Total

Beer variety seeking — 39%

"I love to experiment with different styles of beer."

Beer taste preferences — 20%

"I prefer beer with a strong, full-bodied taste."

Beer engagement — 16%

"I see myself drinking more beer in the future than I do today."

Overall alcoholic beverage interest — 16%

Overall beverage interest — 9%

Category engagement

Consumer demographics include household composition, marital status, education, and employment.

Source: TCG analysis by Claire Zhou, Dimitar Antor, and Linda Deeken.

Emotion is why the vast majority of superconsumers are likely to remain superconsumers from year to year unless some kind of life event triggers them to change their behavior (figure 1-5). The family-oriented cheese superconsumer is likely to buy lots of cheese until the kids go off to college, and the marathon-running Gatorade superconsumer is likely to buy Gatorade products by the handful until he has less time to exercise because his family is growing or until age catches up with him.

Considering how fragmented the consumer landscape is, how diverse—ethnically, economically, and emotionally—consumers are, and how quickly things change, the stability

FIGURE 1-5

Superconsumer stability year after year (What percentage of beer superconsumers in 2013 were still superconsumers in subsequent years?)

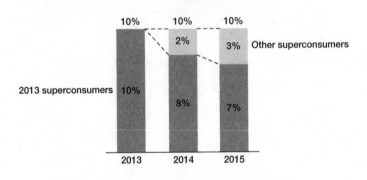

Source: TCG analysis by Claire Zhou, Dimitar Antor, and Linda Deeken.

of superconsumers is increasingly important. As long as you treat them well and offer them what they want, you can count on them to keep coming back for more.

Their dependability also helps improve forecasting. Imprecise market forecasts can be wildly destructive to profit if you produce too much and have to sell it at massive markdowns or if you underproduce and miss out on sales. A report by the auditing company KPMG and the Economist Intelligence Unit revealed that only 1 percent of 580 companies hit their forecast exactly over a three-year period, and only 22 percent were within 5 percent.[1] On average, companies were off by 13 percent, an inaccuracy that had an estimated 6 percent impact on total shareholder value.

Beyond their buying power and predictability, superconsumers can also offer wisdom and new insights about products. Their interest in new uses and variations is very helpful to businesses looking to ramp up their own innovation efforts.

These insights can prove invaluable. Since superconsumers know what they want and are a great test audience, they take much of the risk out of innovation and allow businesses to experiment more and take more chances.

The wise input of superconsumers also allows you to tap into a whole other category of consumers called *potential superconsumers.* This group is as passionate as superconsumers but doesn't spend as much. Potential superconsumers represent 20 percent of a category's consumer base, and they respond well to the same advertising, marketing, and product innovations that superconsumers do.

Companies that use superconsumers' insights to refine their decision making ultimately grow sales and margins across all segments. And this pattern of profitable growth emerges in a wide variety of industries and geographic locations. One summer, I discovered it worked equally well for both a bank in the European debt capital markets and a company selling frozen treats for children in the United States. Superconsumers consistently have a positive impact, regardless of the company's rank, size, resources, or business model.

My point is, superconsumers can work for you, too. And it's not hard to make success happen. For the most part, superconsumers exist for whatever your business is selling. They're already buying your products or services. So the key is to find these valuable consumers, through social media and data analysis, and to listen to them and engage with them (see the sidebar "Five Characteristics of Superconsumers"). Just as Sally served as a powerful north star for the office-supply manufacturer, superconsumers can be your guide for simple, superior, and sustainable growth.

Five Characteristics of Superconsumers

They're more than just heavy users with a new name. Unlike traditional heavy users, superconsumers combine big spending with high engagement and deep interest in new uses for a product.

They exist in every business. Our data suggests that they exist in most consumer packaged-goods categories and in many other markets as well.

They're emotionally invested. If you talk to superconsumers, you'll learn that most have very logical reasons for their behavior. They simply find more meaning and benefits in a given category than other customers do. In fact, just about everyone is a superconsumer of something.

They're easier to find. Big data and social media enable you to identify them.

They're willing to buy even more . . . and lead others to follow them. Superconsumers account for at least three times as much growth as other consumers do. And they influence millions through social media and word of mouth.

FROM OFFICE SCISSORS TO A QUEST FOR CREATIVITY

To get an idea of how superconsumers evolve, let's look at how an average consumer was transformed into a superconsumer. Although each superconsumer is a different person with unique emotions and goals, their journeys tend to follow the path depicted in figure 1-6.

FIGURE 1-6

The making of a superconsumer

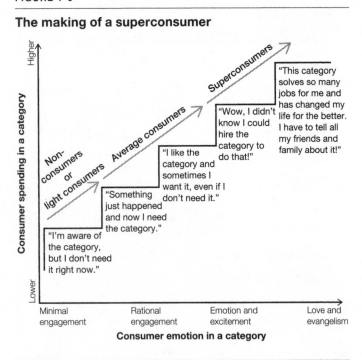

Here's a summary of the journey that the figure shows: average consumers begin their transformations into superconsumers after being triggered by some sort of life event, which awakens a series of otherwise dormant emotions, motivations, and desires. After their passions are stoked and the consumers continue to expose themselves to the category and educate themselves about it, they may become full-on superconsumers. From that point on, they may seek out a community of other superconsumers and spread their passion to others.

For example, my wife, Kristen, was transformed from a nonconsumer to an average consumer to a superconsumer of scissors. I'm using my wife as a subject because I know her well, of course, but also because she's a good example of how superconsumers are often hiding in plain sight among our families and friends. These people can serve as great resources if you're new to the superconsumer phenomenon and you want to learn more before implementing these ideas in your business.

For most of her life, Kristen was a nonconsumer of scissors. Sure, she had used them as a student, but she had no need to buy or shop for them.

But a major life event changed all that. When we bought our first condominium in 2002, we decided to use the extra bedroom as an office. With the new office,

Kristen now needed office supplies. Had we not moved into a new home with an office, I don't think we would have made the trip to the store. So Kristen was a perfectly average consumer of scissors. No amount of advertising would have swayed her to buy more scissors. Even if she had gone to a retailer that offered her a 90 percent discount on a pair, she would not have bought another pair.

The situation changed in 2003, after Kristen attended a scrapbooking party and came home having spent $100 on scissors—*multiple* pairs of scissors. Each pair, she explained, allowed her to cut different shapes from paper. Thankfully, I was too confused to argue. This formative experience to observe, accept, and not judge superconsumer behavior helped me in my career—and my marriage.

The party had riled up some dormant emotions, desires, and motivations that would simmer under the surface for years. Soon after the party, we were expecting the first of our three kids. With the arrival of this first child, Kristen left her job as an oncology and intensive-care nurse. But she missed working with her hands, creative problem solving, and the sense of purpose she derived from her job, and crafting was a great replacement (both practices involve needles). Like many stay-at-home parents, she was often frustrated by the Sisyphean nature of raising young children. So she "hired" scissors, in a sense—and other scrapbooking products—to provide her with the feeling of forward progress, which she used to feel when a patient got better and went home from the hospital.

She also found it very satisfying to create something aesthetically pleasing. One Christmas, she made dozens of snowflakes via a method called quilling. When I asked her why she spent so much time on it, she simply answered, "Because they are beautiful."

Her journey to becoming a superconsumer was also helped along by her family. Kristen is a fourth-generation Japanese American, and the importance of aesthetics and presentation is baked into her Japanese heritage. She has fond memories of doing arts and crafts as a little girl with her late grandmother, Eunice Nagatani, who made little cloth dolls by hand and sold them at local fairs. Eunice had a strong belief that people were put on the earth to work, and through her work ethic, she brought joy to others. Kristen always remembered this.

At face value, it would be very hard to explain why our household went from spending less than $5 on scissors in 2002 to about $100 a few years later. The condominium purchase and home office conversion caused us to enter the category. The scrapbooking party—exposure, education, and experience—unlocked some dormant emotions and motivations. But Kristen also needed another life-stage trigger—quitting her job and dealing with the ins and outs of being a stay-at-home mom—and her memories of her grandmother's crafting to trigger her emotional desire to spend $100 on scissors (figure 1-7). The combination of life-stage triggers; inherent motivations; and exposure, education, and experience created a superconsumer of scissors.

But Kristen's evolution as a superconsumer does not end there. As her skills continue to grow, she has embraced new crafting challenges and spends much more money than just the $100 on scissors. Her record is $50 on one pair of scissors—something called a rotary scissors for use with fabric. She has converted a spare bedroom in our house into her crafting workshop. She taps into the broader crafting community on YouTube, Pinterest, Etsy, and other places for inspiration. She is very receptive and eager to try new and innovative products.

Kristen is, without a doubt, a crafting superconsumer. She is deeply involved in crafting and spends a lot on it; as an active social-media user, she's relatively easy to find; and, most of all, she is knowledgeable and has strong opinions.

Concerning the last attribute, if a scissors company reached out to her to help it optimize its marketing, sales,

FIGURE 1-7

Combination of life-stage triggers; inherent motivations; and exposure, education, and experience to create a superconsumer of scissors

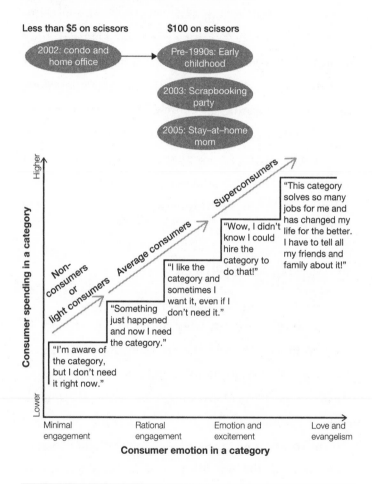

and innovation strategy, she could surely help the company execute a simpler, speedier, and more certain path to profitable growth. If the same company wanted to reinvent the rules of how to win in the scissors category—say, a subscription service to the latest crafting scissors and other crafting products—she could help the company know which rules to break and which to preserve. If entrepreneurs wanted her advice on creating an entirely new category for her quest, she could definitely help them lead the way.

And, like all superconsumers, Kristen's passion and wisdom—and her spending, too, let's be honest—is what makes her so beneficial to businesses.

THE BENEFITS OF CLARITY

If I had to offer just one word to describe the benefit of superconsumers, I would choose *clarity*. Superconsumers offer clear solutions to complex problems. And this capability will be particularly important when it's time to implement your strategy.

If you've ever tried to move your team or organization in a new strategic direction, then you're probably well aware of how hard it is. Often, the strategy is clear to the team who came up with it, but not so clear or compelling to the rest of the leadership. The hard part is getting buy-in from important stakeholders, receiving the right amount of funds and resources, and convincing different parts of the organization to get behind the idea. Leaders will not change their behavior unless the strategy is crystal clear. If you can't explain your strategy in thirty seconds, you won't win over your leaders. And if you can't explain your strategy in thirty seconds to the rest of the organization, your message won't stick and they won't execute your strategy.

But since a superconsumer strategy is a simple idea, you'll have an easier time communicating it with your cross-functional leaders and convincing them to follow it. The very simplicity of the strategy can relieve a lot of the pain, resistance, and stress (but not all of it, of course!) that managers tend to feel when trying to execute a strategy.

Superconsumers bring clarity via big-data credibility. In my experience, a superconsumer strategy tends to reduce much of the guesswork that is common with other consumer-centric approaches. Since superconsumers are such a small segment of consumers and have such extreme emotions, economics, and behaviors, they tend to stand out sharply in your data sets. When a leader sees superconsumers—and their value—clearly in the company's current big data, he or she is more likely to recognize how superconsumers can improve the business.

First off, the data speaks for itself: superconsumers spend more overall and pay a higher average price per unit. They do so because they pay for higher-end brands and higher-priced products and because they have less of a tendency to buy volume through special discounts and other promotions. All of these habits translate into higher margins, which increase your ROI. If you can present this argument in a visual way, you're bound to get people's attention.

Consider the frozen-pizza market. Figure 1-8, as simple as it is, says it all. And charts like this one aren't based on conjecture. They present simple data that shows the

FIGURE 1-8

Frozen-pizza superconsumer economics, sales and profitability share

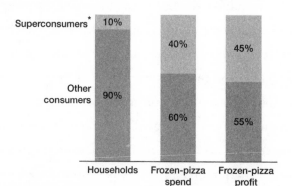

*Superconsumers pay 5 percent more per pound, and companies spend 33 percent less on promotions to superconsumers.
Source: Nielsen and TCG analysis.

current impact of superconsumers. It's relatively easy to compile similar data for your own business to help convince others—especially your chief financial officer (CFO)—that superconsumers are a safe group to bet on.

Because superconsumers are like superdelegates in a US presidential election—that is, small in number, but with more clout than other consumers have—they also make it easier for cross-functional leaders to make decisions and allocate resources. Most functional leaders have a good idea about the costs and advantages of different options, but knowing precisely how superconsumers behave will often lend more clarity to whatever decisions they have to make.

For example, one of our clients discovered that its superconsumers were shopping exclusively at two very distinct kinds of retailers—convenience stores and dollar stores—which represented 50 percent of the sales and even higher profit. Because of the data, each functional group was willing to pivot because it saw a clear path to growth. The sales group could more precisely realign its sales force and promotion budgets, and those in charge of procurement, manufacturing, and distribution could operate more efficiently instead of devoting much of their resources to big retailers, which were challenging to deal with. The big retailers required a lot of inventory, and our client struggled to get an accurate sense of consumer demand, the client often had to deal with idle manufacturing lines or excess inventory that had to be discounted or thrown out.

The superconsumer framework made life much simpler for everyone involved. Our client narrowed its focus on superconsumers, studied their behaviors, and based its decisions on those behaviors.

This is what superconsumers do: they separate signal from noise. If the sales group knows where superconsumers are geographically concentrated, it can more easily prioritize certain regions over others. If your supply chain has the same information, it should have a better idea of which plant and distribution channels it should upgrade and how to reinvest its scarce capital expenditure budget. And if marketing knows where to find superconsumers, it can optimize its resources to reach them, which can have a big impact. With the help of Crown Media, my partner Chris Fosdick conducted a study on how twenty-five popular consumer packaged-goods brands spent their cable-media dollars across ninety-nine cable channels. What they found was startling: only 10 percent of each company's cable-media spending was reaching its category superconsumers. If these brands shifted 10 to 20 percent of their media buying toward programs that their superconsumers were watching, the companies could drive 4 to 5 percent sales growth while holding total media dollars flat.

Of course, your company might be nowhere near the size of the big packaged-goods companies, but superconsumers can affect your business just the same. If you are a startup or an up-and-coming company, superconsumers can be the core mission and purpose of your company. Because most startups grow out of a consumer's yearning for something better, they are already full of superconsumers. *Inc.* magazine published the mission statements of thirty startups valued at over $1 billion.[2] The most prevalent theme (80 percent of the startups mentioned it) was to improve the lives of consumers or customers in some way. The next-most-common theme, at 77 percent, was to create the best product or technology. Clearly, these successful startups are aiming to create super-cool stuff for their superconsumers.

On the surface, a superconsumer strategy may seem obvious, especially since you may already have a consumer-centric approach to different aspects of your business. There are a few types of consumer-centric companies. Some companies say they are consumer-centric, but their actions—be it reducing the quality of the product or service or a lack of risk taking to create truly break-through innovation—say the opposite. Another type of consumer-centric company lacks a disciplined process to truly focus on the consumer. Still other companies build a disciplined consumer-centric process, but it is either pointed in the wrong direction (e.g., all consumers) or organized in the wrong sequence. Superconsumers are not the be-all and end-all, but they are the proper place to start a consumer-centric strategy. This point is what many companies miss.

And that disciplined process pointed in the right way and organized in the right sequence is what I hope this book helps you achieve. Through the case studies and practical resources offered throughout the book, I hope that you'll become confident enough to identify and engage your superconsumers—and be inspired by them. And, hopefully, if you listen to these consumers and base your decisions on their feedback, you'll experience more profitable growth.

Part II looks at how three specific companies reinvig-orated their own superconsumer strategies. Let's see how the first company, a major packaged-goods company, did just that with one of its workhorse brands.

part two

HOW THEY DID IT

chapter 2

SIMPLE, SPEEDY STRATEGIES TO WIN: GREAT SNACKS

Many managers at Great Snacks (disguised) believed that their Nacho Cheese brand (disguised) had only moderate growth prospects. Given that the cheese was a lower-priced, processed food in a market in which customers were migrating toward products that were more natural and organic, the managers' ambivalence wasn't surprising. Sure, there were Nacho Cheese fans, but they tended to buy the product only once or twice a year, usually as a dipping sauce for chips, crackers, or vegetables at parties.

But as we began working with Great Snacks and analyzing supermarket scanner and consumer panel data, we discovered a robust segment of superconsumers. In focus groups, these buyers said that they think of Nacho Cheese as a superior cheese. They love the way it melts smoothly and easily, and they have myriad uses for it—uses that range far beyond a dip (one person even claimed to use a little when making a chocolate dessert). After we finished questioning the superconsumers, they traded recipes, emails, and phone numbers with one another, building friendships around their shared passion for Nacho Cheese.

To restart the brand's growth, the company decided to start with these superconsumers, a group whose size we estimated at three million. This was a big shift in strategy. The previous thinking was to identify occasional or former consumers to jump-start growth. But when the members of the Great Snacks team talked to their superconsumers, they learned that their most passionate consumers wanted to use Nacho Cheese more. Not only did the company find growth with its superconsumers, but it also discovered that insights and inspiration from superconsumers could unlock growth with occasional and former users. It was not an either-or strategy but a both-and one. It was about sequence, starting with superconsumers and then having them help unlock the many more potential superconsumers—for Nacho Cheese, a group eight times larger than the three million core—who were waiting to be awoken. Managers believed they had found a viable growth strategy for the first time in years.

Let's follow the Great Snacks team through the process of reinvigorating the Nacho Cheese brand.

A COMFORT-FOOD SUPERCONSUMER: SHARING HER PASSION

Laura (not her real name) is one such superconsumer. She is married with children, and on the surface, she seems no different from any other wife and mother. But as the Great Snacks team got to know her, she became clearly distinctive to the team.

As an extrovert, Laura enjoys people. Her house is a social hub of the neighborhood. Kids are always coming over to hang out. Friends often drop by. And she isn't a lone wolf; her entire family is like this, too. Her husband is a part-time clown.

Laura also loves to cook, and given her role as host extraordinaire, she makes great use of her skills. Clever and creative, she is always looking for inspirational ways to bring joy to others through food. Her personality is evident in her favorite dishes—hearty, family-style dishes that make her friends and family feel warm and welcome, inside and out.

Laura's love for cheese can be summed up in her motto "Cheese is the new ketchup. It's great on most anything." When she was a kid, her parents called her the Mouse, because she was constantly nibbling on blocks of cheese.

Since words are often poor descriptors of one's passion, the Great Snacks team asked Laura to express her feelings about Nacho Cheese through arts and crafts. She made a circular shield, nearly two feet in diameter, which contains everything you would need to know about Laura's relationship with Nacho Cheese. A photo of her family, smiling broadly, is front and center. Surrounding her husband and kids is a wreath made from heart-shaped cutouts of a big bowl of macaroni and cheese. And on the outer rim is what resembles a Micronesian ginger lei that Laura constructed from actual Nacho Cheese labels—thirty, by my count (over $100 worth of cheese). And finally, there's a golden rope, a bow, and a hook for hanging it on a door like holiday wreath.

What causes someone to have this depth of passion? That's the number one question the Great Snacks team posed.

And the answer wasn't clear. Yes, the intersection of Laura's three loves—hosting people, creative cooking, and cheese—predisposes her to making cheese dishes that many people love, but this alone doesn't explain her passion. There are countless other brands of cheese, some of which have much bigger marketing budgets and greater brand awareness than Nacho Cheese. There are also other varieties of cheese, some of which are much more high-end than Nacho Cheese.

So what makes this cheese so special to Laura?

"I know there's a lot of different kinds and brands of cheese out there," Laura said. "I like many of them. But there is nothing quite as ooey, gooey, and drooly as Nacho Cheese. No other cheese melts as perfectly as Nacho Cheese. If a cheese melts too much, it is too liquidy and runs off the plate. If it doesn't melt well enough, it is clumpy, lumpy, and bumpy. It's not special, and the texture doesn't have a good mouthfeel."

She demonstrated this quality in front of the Great Snacks team by dipping a piece of broccoli into a bowl of melted Nacho Cheese. Holding the stalk, she pointed out how the cheese was viscous enough to form a perfect crown on the broccoli's head without falling off the side, yet melty enough to fill every crack and crevice. She then invited the members of the team to dive in, and as they ate, she held court like an art professor explaining the intricacies of color choice and brush strokes in a painting.

Laura also told the team that the cheese helped her solve many common problems that parents know all too well. It makes vegetables more edible for her kids, helps expand their palates, and introduces them to multiculturalism (Nacho Cheese dip with sriracha is outstanding). It also makes Laura's life easier and her budget less expensive. A surprise visit by her daughter and ten of her best friends from the soccer team? Give Laura fifteen minutes, and all of them are satiated with a hot tomato-chili dip.

With Nacho Cheese, Laura has at her disposal dozens of solutions for any meal or social situation. It's versatile, and it has never failed Laura in a clutch. And that's why she spends exponentially more on this cheese than does the average consumer.

LEARNING FROM SUPERCONSUMERS

Like many organizations, Great Snacks saw its brands and products somewhat differently than how its superconsumers saw them. There are a few reasons for this difference.

Executives consider products and brands from the lens of the supply chain—which ingredients go into a product and how it is made, distributed, and sold. So it's not hard to imagine how the team didn't recognize Nacho Cheese as on trend. They saw it for what it was, an industrial mass of cheese versus what it was not, finely sliced or shredded cheese. Nacho Cheese does not need refrigeration, whereas most cheese does. The product is often sold in the center of the store—a location that is struggling to grow—whereas most other cheeses are sold in the perimeter of the store, an area that is growing. Nacho Cheese is American, not European or exotic.

In contrast, consumers see brands and products from the opposite end of the spectrum: How do I use it, who is it for, and what benefits does it give me? In terms of Nacho Cheese, superconsumers such as Laura see the product as a hot mess of a cheese that is worth paying a big premium for.

This is where Daniel Zein (disguised), the CFO of Great Snacks, was instrumental. A global citizen, Zein loves many kinds of premium cheeses, and it wouldn't be far-fetched to think he would dismiss Nacho Cheese.

Interestingly, the unique collection of experiences led him to the same conclusion as Laura's—Nacho Cheese was special. As CFO, Zein first noticed how much pricing power the Nacho Cheese brand had. Being well versed in the complexity and volatility of commodity costs, he understood the value of pricing power to weather commodity costs swings. The company's cheese product had minimal private-label competition in a category where private label was large and growing. Finally, as a cheese superconsumer himself, he noticed the textural uniqueness of Nacho Cheese, its incredible melt. He recognized that the creaminess of the cheese had much in common with high-end cheeses that were growing twice as fast and for nearly double the price per pound.

Zein thought that Nacho Cheese could be one of the company's most valuable brands, so he encouraged the team to dig further into the product. The team did some robust analysis, and to their surprise, they discovered that Nacho Cheese's consumers spanned the entire income spectrum.

From the data, it was obvious that Nacho Cheese could be a much bigger brand. Of all the full meals that consumers eat at home, about 37 percent are consumed hot and include cheese. But Nacho Cheese was used in only a fraction of those meals. To grow its product, the Great

Snacks team decided to focus on the twenty-four million or so other consumers who share the same three loves that Laura had—people, cooking, and cheese—but who may not understand the magic of Nacho Cheese and the dozens of life solutions that it could deliver.

Simply put, the team gathered data from their superconsumers, ensured that the resultant insights and inspiration also appealed to the other twenty-four million consumers, and then geared its marketing, innovation, and retail execution to their tastes and behaviors. The immediate challenge was to convince the company leadership that Nacho Cheese could grow through better marketing and innovation—from packaging to product.

Line extensions into other forms of cheese were also a logical action step. Great Snacks drove growth by megabranding Nacho Cheese into other categories. The core business grew steadily faster than inflation, but the extensions in cheese (e.g., slices, shredded cheese) grew by double digits. All told, the brand extensions drove more than $50 million in growth, and the megabrand grew $100 million in three years.

For years, innovation for Nacho Cheese was a challenge. Since the brand was not well understood, innovation concepts yielded mixed results, which made the team hesitant to pursue breakthrough innovation. But with new data, the team revamped its innovation testing process to include both superconsumers (like Laura) and potential superconsumers (folks who could become like Laura). The group was pleasantly surprised to find that among all the new product concepts it tested, some were off-the-charts positive for superconsumers. The team made a few tweaks, the new concepts tested positive for potential superconsumers as well, and the team finally had the results it needed to proceed.

The team saw that retail activation was inconsistent across retailers. In some stores, Nacho Cheese was placed in the center of the store. In others, it was refrigerated in the cheese and dairy section. So the team did some analysis and found that Nacho Cheese sold faster in the refrigerated section, which consequently produced better results for Great Snacks and the retailer. The team learned that superconsumers strongly preferred the product when it was sold in the refrigerated section. What's more, potential superconsumers had a much easier time finding it in the refrigerated section.

Finally, the Great Snacks team used big data to uncover meaningful ways of improving marketing ROI. It used big data from Nielsen Catalina Solutions—a joint such as websites, magazines, and social-media channels.

Marketing mix: By using a mixed-modeling program such as Mix 2.0, which processes data in seven days or so, you can quickly gain information about your performance (say, your performance over the holidays) and optimize your near-future campaigns (e.g., Mother's Day or Easter). The faster cycle time also allows you to conduct small test-and-learn experiments with superconsumers. Instead of running one big national campaign, you can run different [...] different superconsumer geograph[...] can run multiple advertising [...] geting superconsumers a[...] The results come fast enoug[...] to optimize for one big nationa[...] you should stay at regional camp[...]

Additionally, multitouch attributi[...] allows you to measure the ROI of a digi[...] campaign at the individual level. This fine[...]

---

venture that creates a single-source panel of consumers from the sixty million loyalty-card holders from grocery stores and the Nielsen TV panel of two to three million households. The single-source data gave the team interesting insights on the actual TV shows that Nacho Cheese aficionados were watching. In one test using this data, the team found that superconsumers were fifteen times more responsive to Nacho Cheese advertising than other consumers! The vice president of marketing noted that the brand's marketing objective was to have a conversation with superconsumers about their love for Nacho Cheese, but to do so in a way that potential superconsumers could listen in.

The beauty of all this was that the data the team used to improve innovation, retail activation, and marketing was already there. Superconsumers gave the marketers a way to synthesize the data into a coherent and coordinated set of actions and metrics. Looking at superconsumers like Laura, the team gained confidence that the strategy had even more upside. And the team saw the potential and ran with it.

For a summary of how these approaches could work in your own business, see the sidebar "Let Superconsumers Improve Your Marketing ROI."

Let Superconsumers Improve Your Marketing ROI

Globally, Nielsen estimates that for every $1.00 spent on advertising, companies reap a median of $0.66 in gross profit. There are three practical ways to improve this ROI: media buying, marketing mix, and messaging. Superconsumers can help you with all three.

Media buying: Thanks to big data from Nielsen Catalina Solutions, which merges a database of sixty million loyalty-card shoppers and the multimillion-household Nielsen TV panel, we know that many major companies are misspending their advertising budgets.

In many cases, brands could increase their sales by an estimated 2 to 3 percent while holding their media budgets flat just by better allocating their dollars to programs and channels that focus on reaching superconsumers—rather than e... more cost-effectively. And there's ... approach wouldn't apply to...

data enables you to compare your success with superconsumers with your success with other consumers and to recalibrate as necessary.

Messaging: Word of mouth from one consumer to another is becoming more powerful and credible, especially with millennials. By finding superconsumers and evaluating their behavior through analytics, you can continually refine your message to better suit their wants and needs, and you increase brand awareness in the process.

LESSONS LEARNED

We can learn a few lessons from the Great Snacks superconsumer strategy. Let's look at some of them now.

Find Passion

So many brands try to create passion where it does not exist. On the other hand, many brands ignore emotion in pursuit of profit. Perhaps the smartest thing for a brand to do is to find the passion that already exists and embrace it. Brands such as Nacho Cheese that do this in the right sequence—passion first, then profit—and in the right way, through superconsumers who bridge the gap between passion and profit, don't need to compromise between engaging emotionally with the consumer and striving for profit.

Look for the Overlooked

Some brands and businesses are always undervalued more for perception than reality. Undervaluation does not happen because managers are not smart. More often, managers are too far removed from their consumers and either don't use their own products or don't intimately know someone who does. They're not empathetic enough. At Great Snacks, once the leaders tasted Nacho Cheese, they instantly understood its opportunity. If you find yourself in this situation and are trying to convince your organization to change its mindset, of course you want to be prepared with the facts. But you also need to engineer an experience that engenders empathy. Have the leaders talk to a superconsumer or watch a video of one. Have them experience the product itself. They need to feel it, not just take your word for it.

Be Curious

Where there is smoke, there is probably fire. The leaders who are the most successful at growing businesses owe their achievement not to an abundance of answers, but to an abundance of questions. The secret is not creating the epiphany, but wondering about an epiphany in others. Through social-media analysis, the Great Snacks team saw that superconsumers used the cheese product year round, which ran counter to the overall spiky seasonality of the business. And they wondered why superconsumers used the cheese so frequently and if others might want to do so as well.

Think Both-And, *Not Just* Either-Or

Some accurate observations lay behind the perceptions that had held Nacho Cheese back: organic is on trend, and Nacho Cheese is not organic. If the Great Snacks team members had solely used an either-or mindset, they wouldn't have invested more in Nacho Cheese, because it wasn't on trend. However, with a both-and approach, they saw that their nonorganic brand could grow. In other words, instead of asking what was true, they asked what would need to be true. They needed latent demand, pricing power, and brand strength. Since they had all three, they decided to move forward.

The key behind these lessons is to recognize that consumers are wonderfully complex and endlessly surprising—they're humans, after all. They have beliefs and preferences that are different from yours. Their behaviors are complicated. And most of all, they have rich emotions that even they may not fully understand.

So you need to find these consumers and listen to them. They exist in every category, and they have a lot to say.

chapter 3

BREAKING THE RULES TO WIN: EASY GROCERY

Like many neighborhood stores that have grown into regional brands, Easy Grocery (disguised) experienced its fair share of growth and plateaus. When it built more stores and began acquiring local competitors, it grew steadily and became a strong regional brand that achieved relatively high scale.

To grow the stores further, the strategy team had to invest in improving numerous areas across the store experience—decor, lighting, uniforms, layout—while still offering good prices and promotions. The strategy worked. By creating high-end stores with a welcoming ambiance and using the stores' quality as a marketing angle, the team increased trips and traffic, which drove strong short-term results.

But the grocery industry is highly competitive, and there were other companies that had more stores and more scale. They also had an even better assortment of goods, offered better store experiences, and held more pricing power.

Easy Grocery was stuck in the middle, so it turned to its superconsumers.

The team at Easy Grocery knew that it had a strong private-label business—products and services sold under its own brand name—and a very loyal following of private-label superconsumers. Now, a private label, in its own right, wasn't unique to Easy Grocery; every grocery store sells private-label products, usually at lower prices and lower quality than name brands. But because of the loyalty and passion of private-label superconsumers—who made up 15 percent of Easy Grocery's customers—these shoppers drove 50 percent of the store's private-label sales and an even higher share of its total store sales. For Easy Grocery, total store sales were much higher than other stores' sales, so the company executives decided to leverage the store's private-label superconsumers as much as they could.

The first step was understanding these superconsumers better. Through research, the strategy team found that they came in two distinct types: disciplined deal seekers and treasure hunters. The next step was finding out more about both.

Michelle (not her real name), a disciplined deal seeker, is not a robotic price chaser who couldn't care less about quality. A discerning shopper, she cares deeply about what she provides for her family. She's disciplined because she has a specific quest in mind: to save enough money to buy a house. But because she doesn't want to cut corners for her family, her job was to find good-quality products at great prices.

"I love Easy Grocery," Michelle told us. "As much as I could, I exclusively shopped Easy Grocery's private-label brands for nine months. I saved a ton of money from buying private label and put that into my savings account. I did this in several areas of my life. This allowed us to save enough for a down payment on a house we now own. We bought our house without really changing our lifestyle, because Easy Grocery's product quality was great. So

I didn't feel guilty, because I wasn't cutting corners for my children. Easy Grocery was a big part of that."

Michelle's decision to buy Easy Groceries' private label almost exclusively was deeply emotional. The affinity she felt was as deep and personal as I've seen in consumers of some of the world's most powerful luxury and lifestyle brands.

Then there was Sandy (not her real name), a treasure hunter. Unlike Michelle, she wasn't seeking cheaper versions of products that she knew well. She was seeking great products at a good price. Her job was to find unique ingredients, new ethnic foods, and new food and beverage categories. Her quest was to explore the world and take her family on a culinary adventure. And Sandy was willing to travel to a variety of grocery stores to find something new.

From a conversation with her mother, Sandy was excited to discover that Easy Grocery stocked several brands that sold a unique assortment of goods. And while she still shopped at other grocery stores, her loyalty to Easy Grocery kept growing as she found the everyday items she needed. What's more, because Easy Grocery provided so much variety, she eventually shopped there exclusively, to save time and money.

While both Michelle and Sandy buy many private-label brands, they have very different needs and wants. This is where Easy Grocery's wider portfolio of private-label brands came in handy. Of the dozen or so private-label brands the store carried, about half were geared toward Michelle and other disciplined deal seekers. The other half were geared toward Sandy and other treasure hunters.

With this knowledge, Easy Grocery took the shopper-level purchase data from both types of super-consumers and married it with motivational and emotional data from the same shoppers to build a precision private-label database. Easy Grocery knew which stores had more Michelles and which had more Sandys. With this information, the retailer could tailor the stores to each type of superconsumer and thereby maximize its marketing opportunities. Through data-mining, they found four million more deal-seeking, price-driven, private-label superconsumers like Michelle and another four million treasure-hunting, private-label superconsumers like Sandy.

Thanks to this deeper understanding of their most valuable shoppers, Easy Grocery executives were empowered to experiment with new brands and products. Several executives were seasoned marketers from the best consumer packaged-goods companies. From their earlier experience at those companies, they discovered that the traditional rules about brands and innovation were flexible. And they could break some established rules as well.

MAKING PRIVATE LABEL INTO A PREMIUM PRODUCT

Most grocers play with private labels in some way, as these products generate a higher profit margin, sometimes 20 to 25 percent higher, according to a Dartmouth study.[1] But stores are often careful not to bite the hand that feeds them—namely, their branded suppliers—and not to go head-to-head with mainstream products at mainstream prices. Most retailers choose to come in at lower quality and lower prices, so the term *premium private label* seems like an oxymoron to them.

Easy Grocery inverted this logic and created higher-quality premium private-label brands at higher prices than many mainstream products, which was a stretch for a chain that wasn't playing in the high end of the market. The grocer chose organic food and beverages, which didn't upset its suppliers, because the manufacturers of branded consumer packaged goods were not in the organic-product line. And since the team knew that an increasing number of consumers (including the grocer's own private-label superconsumers) were feeling concerned about transparency in their food but could not afford to eat organic across all categories, the marketers believed that a move into organic, private-label products was a safe, if not advantageous, bet.

Easy Grocery could make this move because of its private-label superconsumers, especially the disciplined deal seekers, who viewed organic, premium private-label products as a great way to feed their families healthy meals and save money.

Considering the superconsumer demand for organic and the lack of competition in this space, the members of the Easy Grocery team had a clear road map for product innovation and brand building. They made sure that their products were made with only natural ingredients— that is, no artificial ingredients (real or perceived)—and minimal processing, and that there were no antibiotics, hormones, or nitrates in their meat products or rBST (artificial bovine somatotropin hormone) in the brand's milk. And they made sure that consumers could spot the brand promise on the packaging in ten seconds or less.

They also launched multiple products at scale and with minimal advertising by using loyalty-card and digital apps (which were mostly downloaded by their superconsumers) to precisely reach the superconsumers. And the brand grew at four times the rate of overall organic growth.

Once Easy Grocery successfully created a premium private-label brand in the organic and natural category, it became easier to extend those brands and to launch other premium brands in other areas, such as farm-fresh dairy. The grocer also created premium lifestyle brands with targeted consumer benefits, such as "for moms, by moms," which was a great way to reach its treasure-hunter, private-label superconsumers.

TAKING MORE RISKS

Easy Grocery had hired several successful and seasoned marketers from large consumer packaged-goods companies, an increasing trend. But in the rapidly changing environment of grocery marketing, these new leaders and the rest of the team knew that a marketing-as-usual approach could sink the stores. They had to take some risks. The new leaders were even more successful at Easy Grocery because the superconsumers they knew from their earlier positions provided the team with additional benefits when it came to innovation.

Speed

The Easy Grocery team searched for trends across categories and then quickly based some hypotheses for potential innovation on the purchase patterns of the private-label superconsumers. This strategy was a change for many of the executives. In their prior lives at other companies, innovation processes took years to launch because the companies spent much time, effort, and money perfecting a product before its launch, to minimize the risk. But Easy Grocery launched new products in a matter of months because of the insights it had gleaned from superconsumers. A superconsumer—who spends more and cares more than other consumers do—can identify winning products and losing products before their launch and can offer suggestions for products that are not quite ready to go to market.

In this way, superconsumers helped Easy Grocery hone its message. Since the company had no big marketing dollars to tell the world about its innovations, the grocer's new products had to be able to show a shopper their benefits in ten seconds or less. A study in Australia noted that for routine products like milk, shoppers spend only fourteen to seventeen seconds at the shelf.[2] But even for the high

63

end of the spectrum—hair care products—the time was still less than a minute. The ten-second rule meant that the benefit had to be so obvious or so compelling that no advertising or promotion was necessary. Although an average consumer might struggle with this exercise, which could lead Easy Grocery to dismiss too many ideas, super-consumers were up to the challenge. And if these devoted consumers were swayed by the message, the new company knew that the new product had a higher likelihood of success. (See the sidebar "How to Attract Their Attention" for more thoughts on finding a message that grabs consumers quickly.)

How to Attract Their Attention

The average shopper spends less than a minute scanning any particular shelf in the grocery store. However, most shelves are designed for the lowest common denominator and are focused on highlighting price or the most convenient choice. Few merchandising strategies are designed with superconsumers in mind—both the consumers' everyday jobs and their ultimate quests.

Consider a clever florist who found a compelling way to merchandise flowers to men on Valentine's Day. Rather than creating a sign that advertised its flowers, the florist hung a banner that targeted the job that men were tasked with—making their partners happy—with a direct question: "How mad is she?" The sign also provided a series of multiple choices: *A* was a single rose, *B* was a half dozen, *C* was a dozen, and so on. It was clever way to focus on the task at hand in a humorous way.

You can apply the same thinking to superconsumers. Find out what they're "hiring" your products for and what their quest is, and address both.

By speeding up these two processes—the time to launch for new products and the time to convey the product's message—through its interactions with superconsumers, the Easy Grocery team was able to identify ideas and execute them much faster.

Focus on Fixing, Not Perfecting

Because of the dedication and loyalty of its superconsumers, the Easy Grocery team could refine and tweak its products postlaunch.

Instead of prelaunch tests that ask potential consumers to imagine their use of a product, the team preferred real data from real consumers who actually had hands-on experience with the products. In this way, the consumers were in a better position to offer suggestions. Although postlaunch testing meant that Easy Grocery was launching less-than-perfect products, the team members believed that the superconsumer-focused learning they could gain from this approach would lower the risk of long-term failure.

Ultimately, Easy Grocery traded analysis paralysis for speed and the confidence to offer its superconsumers a potentially imperfect product to start—a product the grocer could quickly perfect with superconsumer input. This is a key reason its innovation success rate was three times the success rate of the industry.

Freedom from Conventional Approaches

Innovators at Easy Grocery were unshackled. Not only could they see where the leading manufacturers were headed, but they also had their own fact base of strong innovations and postlaunch learning. They started to see white-space opportunities that neither they nor the leading brands were pursuing. The only thing holding

Easy Grocery back was the conventional wisdom that private-label retailers were followers, not leaders.

Since the grocer had already broken the rules, it decided to break this one as well. Easy Grocery was the first to market with frozen Greek yogurt desserts. It was the first to market with a specialty, high-end line of Mexican frozen foods. It also launched the first megabrand that spanned multiple food philosophies, from calorie counting to protein seeking or gluten-free.

One the one hand, much of the grocer's freedom came from its business model as a retailer. It could identify and launch innovations free from the restrictions and baggage of a singular brand. And it could prioritize any category it wanted to. It was free of the constraints of existing manufacturing assets. The freedom to be brand agnostic, category agnostic, and asset agnostic enabled Easy Grocery to be consumer-centric.

But the reality for many big companies is that the world is changing, and more companies will have to become more agnostic to survive. According to Nielsen, the twenty-five largest food and beverage companies in 2015 drove 45 percent of category sales in the United States but generated only 3 percent of the total category growth—roughly $1 billion in sales out of $35 billion in category growth.[3] That is a 0.1 percent compound annual growth rate (CAGR). Private labels drove 23 percent of the growth ($8 billion) and grew at 2.6 percent CAGR, driven by these private-label superconsumers. Entrepreneurs are also relatively agnostic of brand, category, and assets. This explains the long tail you would see in a graph comparing the number of companies and category growth: twenty thousand companies below the hundred largest companies drove 49 percent of all category growth ($17 billion), growing at a 6.3 percent CAGR. As these numbers show, it's much easier to lead when you are not constrained by conventional name-brand practice.

LESSONS LEARNED

Easy Grocery's willingness to break the rules helped build a multibillion-dollar private-label business that would be one of the largest consumer packaged-goods manufacturers in the United States. Despite the grocer's success, it may be unwise to believe that every rule can be broken. Here are some lessons to consider.

"Premiumization" Is Possible

While it's extremely difficult for a value or mainstream brand to become a full-on premium retailer, these brands can play in premium parts of the market. Easy Grocery was able to do this by using superconsumers to figure how to deliver benefits that exceeded the product's price, which exceeded the grocer's costs.

You can follow Easy Grocery's approach in your own market. Use your superconsumers to figure out which benefits are unmet. Then charge them a price that is both fair to them and exceeds your cost to deliver it. An important bit of context to keep in mind is that superconsumers' frame of reference is likely much bigger than what is on the shelf in front of them. For example, you can double the price of coffee in a grocery store and still be a "value" to a coffee shop like Starbucks if the products deliver comparable benefits. As long as this equation holds true, any company can play in nearly any price tier in the market.

Smarter Risk Taking Is Possible

Superconsumers can dramatically decrease the cost of failure. You can learn from them more rapidly, which means you can test, learn, and improve a product as you go. No more unnecessary planning and perfecting. Under Armour was launched and perfected with the University of Maryland football team (athletic gear superconsumers). Keurig was perfected in offices (the location of coffee superconsumers) before it ever sold a machine to consumers.

Breaking the Rules Is Encouraged

Some conventional wisdom is still wise, as rules were established for a logical reason at some point, but some of these rules may be based on assumptions that are no longer true. The key is to look for rules that shouldn't be broken on their own but that create new opportunities when broken as a group. Easy Grocery simultaneously broke two rules by launching a premium product that also offered a lot of value. The same goes for Ball Park. Its angus beef hot dogs were premium products compared with regular beef hot dogs, but still a value over expensive kosher hot dogs. Bud Light Lime was a higher-quality beverage than Bud Light, but offered more value than Corona. New products that credibly deliver both premium and value can be very successful.

Another tip is to overcome one consumer hurdle by solving another relevant hurdle instead. I call this *barrier bartering.* Imagine if your cable company created an original movie. Would you want to watch? Probably not, because the consumer belief is that the quality will not be good. Netflix solved its quality hurdle by solving an equally vexing issue—the cliff-hanger. No matter how good your favorite TV show is, you must often deal with the hassle of waiting a week for the next episode. Netflix successfully created original content (an industry no-no) while simultaneously releasing all episodes of the season at the same time (another industry no-no). Some viewers might have been suspicious of original content from Netflix, but they were willing to try it, knowing that the cliff-hanger problem would go away.

The final tip is to ask what needs to be true. There is a subtle yet significant distinction between asking "Can we do it?" and "What needs to be true so that we can do it?" The first question elicits a binary response of yes or no. Optimists answer yes. Pessimists answer no. Each side believes it is right and disagrees with the other. Because the first question is an opinion question that does not generate new facts, no forward progress is made. However, the second question elicits an open-ended response. Optimists can acknowledge the risks that must be mitigated to justify their optimism. Pessimists can admit that something is possible, as long as they can increase the font on the fine print. New possibilities and prerequisites emerge and create a much higher chance of finding middle ground. Both optimists and pessimists can acknowledge that because the world is changing rapidly, conventional wisdom is following suit. They can agree that the prudent approach is at least to consider what needs to be true if a company were to do something. They can identify the signposts for each scenario and then watch out for these signs.

Consider this basketball analogy. In 2015 the Golden State Warriors were the National Basketball Association (NBA) champions, and their star player, Stephen "Steph" Curry, won the most-valuable-player award. The Warriors are chronic rule breakers, and they embraced paradox. Golden State made more three-point shots than did any other team. What would need to be true for the head coach, Steve Kerr, to allow the players to shoot an abundance of three-pointers in their offense? Mathematically speaking, if the expected value of a three-point shot (that is, the average shooting percentage multiplied by three points) were the same as the expected value of a two-point shot, the coach should not care. Essentially, if your players could shoot three-pointers accurately enough, you would be indifferent or even encourage more three-point shots.

Let's say the average shooting percentage of a two-point shot was 50 percent, so it had an expected value of 1.0 point per shot. Let's also say the average shooting percentage of a three-pointer was 30 percent, so it had an expected value of 0.9 point per shot. Of course, Kerr would encourage more two-point shots. But Kerr has Curry, the league's MVP in 2015 and 2016, with a three-point shooting percentage of 44 percent for his career, which gives him an expected value of 1.3 points per three-pointer. In theory, Curry should shoot as many three-pointers as he can. In the 2016 season, he sank over 400 three-pointers in a single season, which broke his own record of 286 in the prior season. In two years, he will have made more three-pointers than Larry Bird—one of the best shooters in NBA history—made in his entire thirteen-year career. As a supershooter, Steph Curry enabled Coach Kerr to break the conventional wisdom.

In the same way, products and services developed with superconsumers should have a much higher success rate than other offerings, even if the superconsumer-focused approach breaks conventional wisdom, like launching premium private label. Easy Grocery "premiumized" private label just as Golden State embraced a higher-value shot, the three-pointer. Both broke rules by embracing paradox.

Rule breaking may seem scary. But remember two things. Superconsumers are there to help you break the rules. And it is far better to break the rules first, to your advantage, than to have someone else break the rules first and leave you behind.

chapter 4

USING SUPERCONSUMERS TO CREATE NEW CATEGORIES: AMERICAN GIRL

If you have a little girl in your life—a daughter, granddaughter, or niece—you have probably come across the amazing brand that is American Girl. If there was ever a brand with superconsumers, American Girl is it. According to industry estimates, the average American Girl consumer spends yearly on the brand close to half of what they would spend on a smartphone. This spending would represent one of biggest categories of expenditure on children, according to the US Department of Agriculture, right behind health care and clothing.[1]

How is this extreme level of spending possible?

Through the vision of its founder, Pleasant Rowland, American Girl has managed to combine and improve on three categories: toys, multimedia entertainment, and education. The extraordinarily well-crafted dolls, which are eighteen inches tall and portray girls of various ethnicities and socioeconomic backgrounds, are also five to ten times more expensive than your typical doll, especially when you factor in the accessories plus in-store services and experiences (e.g., having tea with your doll, braiding your doll's hair) and all the media for consumption at home (e.g., books, movies, digital sites).

American Girl is also successful because it creates communities of superconsumers in which family members and friends purchase items for girls who own a doll. I know this because Miya, my eldest child, loved American Girl. But what she really loved even more than the dolls were the books, which she read and reread. My wife and I bought many of these for Miya. So did her Aunt Jen. Her cousin, Kaitlin—an even bigger American Girl superconsumer—passed on some of her favorite American Girl dolls to Miya.

But the true American Girl superconsumer is Pauline Oyama, Miya and Kaitlin's grandmother, who used

American Girl as a way to connect with her daughters and granddaughters. American Girl appealed to her on several levels. Since Pauline shared a mutual love of arts and crafts with her daughter and granddaughters, she was attracted to the craftsmanship of American Girl dolls. Also, as someone who had raised three kids and who had a long career as a teacher and Montessori director, she had a keen appreciation for the educational backstory of each doll. Finally, as an empty nester who had left the suburbs for downtown Chicago and who enjoyed memberships to the Goodman Theatre, Chicago Symphony Orchestra, and Lyric Opera of Chicago, she recognized the experiential wonder that is the American Girl store at Water Tower on Magnificent Mile, which makes for truly memorable grandmother-and-granddaughter excursions. These excursions are a big deal for Pauline. They aren't a job or an obligation. They represent a life quest to build family connection.

Thanks to Grandma, both Miya and Kaitlin are potential superconsumers who are highly likely to become actual superconsumers at the appropriate life stage. When you add in aunts and other extended family, Pauline created a super community of superconsumers, or what I call a *super geo*. And just as superconsumers drive a disproportionate amount of profit, super geos are the 10 percent of local markets that can drive 60 percent of the incremental profit pool. In some cases, a 1 percent increase in superconsumers within a super geo can increase total buyers by 10 to 15 percent (beyond superconsumers) and total sales by 20 to 25 percent.

And whenever you have super geos, emotional input from consumers, and personal connection with them, you can create more than just a new brand or new product. You can create a new category.

HOW AMERICAN GIRL LEVERAGES SUPERCONSUMERS

The remarkable success of the American Girl brand offers us a few great insights:

1. Consumers hire brands for a job, but superconsumers hire multiple brands for multiple jobs to solve a quest.

2. Multiple superconsumers near one another (be it physical or psychological proximity) create super geos, where their passion spreads like a virus.

3. Quests enable breakthrough innovations in product offerings. Super geos enable breakthrough

business-model innovation. The presence of both superconsumers and super geos allows you to create new categories.

Creating a new category is the ultimate growth strategy. In a *Harvard Business Review* article, Linda Deeken and I define category creation as bringing together a breakthrough product innovation with a breakthrough business-model innovation.[2] Our study of the *Fortune* 100 fastest-growing companies from 2009 to 2011 shows that category creators constitute only 13 percent of those companies but are responsible for over 50 percent of those years' revenue growth and over 75 percent of the market capitalization growth. A dollar of growth generated by a category creator is valued by Wall Street at four or five times more than an average dollar of growth.

Superconsumers unlock this door. Let's unpack jobs, super geos, and quests, point by point.

HOW QUESTS DIFFER FROM JOBS

Professor Clayton Christensen famously wrote that consumers don't buy products; they hire brands for a job to be done. Pleasant Rowland created a new category of doll-based edutainment that also made gift giving easier. Said differently, she created a new category and business that many related consumers hired for multiple jobs at once.

Let's look at my own family as an example of the various jobs:

1. Miya (daughter) hired American Girl to play with.

2. My wife Kristen (mom) hired American Girl to teach history to Miya.

3. My sister-in-law Jen (aunt) hired American Girl to ensure a successful gift.

4. My mother-in-law Pauline (grandma) hired American Girl to bond over shared experiences.

There are a few big differences between a job and a quest. A job is often something people have to do, whereas a quest is something people want to do. People tend to think of jobs as a nine-to-five experience, but a quest consumes you twenty-four hours a day, seven days a week.

My family did not hire American Girl to do just one job. We hired it for multiple jobs—to build a love for reading, to learn about history, and to play. For me personally, I was hoping American Girl would teach Miya about the real world. She would never know the struggle of my parents as immigrants from war-torn Korea. She would never know what it was like to grow up in a blue-collar home and to do without. My quest was to help Miya avoid growing up entitled and unappreciative of what she has been blessed with.

Stories of hardship, struggle, and yearning are what I most appreciated about American Girl. Take the backstory of Felicity, a horse-loving American Girl who bristles at the customs and constraints women were bound by in Williamsburg, Virginia, circa 1776. Her love of horses is both an expression of love and an expression of independence, which is a microcosm of the broader American Revolution narrative. There's also Kirsten, a Swedish immigrant who now lives in Minnesota. Samantha, an orphan raised by her wealthy grandmother, uses her past hardships and newfound status in life to help others. Kit lives during the Great Depression. And there's Molly, whose father is stationed in England during World War II.

The more Miya played with American Girl, the more she read. And that was awesome for everyone. Miya read literally all the American Girl books and watched all the movies several times over. As every parent knows, telling your children how much harder your life was and how easy they have it is not particularly effective. But having the soil of Miya's imagination tilled with stories of hardship and struggle made it easier for her to understand.

Although my mind was acutely aware of the expense of American Girl, my heart was convinced that this would help me with my quest—no matter what it cost. Heart over mind is the secret to pricing power.

It is tempting to assume that quests are only possible for brands like American Girl or high-engagement categories like toys. But if you look through the eyes of a superconsumer, you see that quests exist all around you, even in mundane categories. The office products superconsumer described earlier in the book also overlaps with superconsumers of The Container Store (organization products). Organization is not only important to this person, but also a thing of beauty. Skin-cleansing superconsumers are also often household-cleaning and laundry superconsumers. One superconsumer described the perfect day as taking a luxurious shower with great fragrances, cleaning the shower while in it, then jumping into freshly laundered pajamas and sliding into a bed with just-laundered sheets. This superconsumer's quest was built on the belief that cleanliness is next to holiness.

HOW SUPER COMMUNITIES (SUPER GEOS) ARE FORMED

As described, a super geo is simply a group of superconsumers who are close enough physically or psychologically to inspire one another and create new superconsumers. The super geo is the primordial soup where demand forms and categories can grow (figure 4-1). Considering how superconsumers are made, a super geo is a contributor to their formation.

A super geo is not necessarily purely based on location. Certainly, the fact that Kaitlin lives half a mile from Miya and that their grandmother is a forty-five-minute drive away does help. But social media allow super geos to be based on mutual interests and common life stages such as motherhood.

While a single superconsumer is powerful, their power grows exponentially when they are close to other people with shared interests and passions. Consider these relevant quotes from Malcolm Gladwell's book

FIGURE 4-1

The making of a super geo

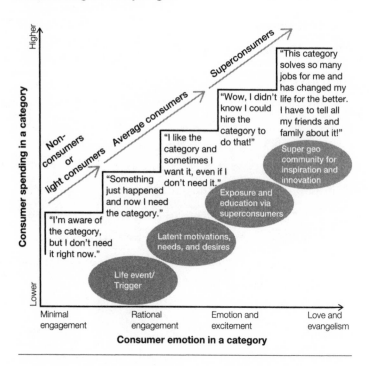

The Tipping Point:

There are exceptional people out there capable of starting epidemics. All you have to do is find them . . .

. . . If you want to bring a fundamental change in people's belief and behavior . . . you needed to create a community around them, where new beliefs can be practiced and expressed and nurtured . . .

... The tipping point is that magic moment when an idea, trend, or social behavior crosses a threshold, tips and spreads like a wildfire.[3]

American Girl was able to quantify the tipping-point idea. While superconsumers behaved relatively the same across different markets, regular consumers spent 20 percent more in markets in which superconsumers were densely clustered in super geos.[4] In effect, superconsumers, especially those who were near one another, were influencing the behavior and decisions of their less passionate peers. You can see this effect is action, for example, when one girl, who has a ton of American Girl products, has a playdate with another girl, who has few such products or none of them. What happens? The second little girl goes home and starts to ask her mommy and daddy (and grandma and auntie) for more.

Tim Joyce (a fellow partner at the Cambridge Group) and Amanda Budow (Nielsen's product lead for digital ratings) did some extensive modeling to quantify drivers of per-capita spending across a wide range of categories and companies. In general, they found that 30 percent of per-capita spending was driven by things that a company can typically control—marketing, innovation, promotions, and so forth. Another 50 percent was driven by market factors like demographics, socioeconomics, traffic, weather, and housing. These were factors not in the company's control, but things it could measure and monitor. The final 20 percent was driven by the density of superconsumers.[5] When you add that 20 percent to the 30 percent you can control, it makes growth strategy a fair fight.

With the influential impact of superconsumers in mind, managers can make better and more cost-effective decisions. The most important area here is having the right performance metric. Most mass-market companies have macro metrics like overall market share to track their performance, and direct-to-consumer businesses generally have micro metrics like ROI and lifetime value at the individual level. Measuring performance at a super-geo level combines the best of both worlds. A point of market share in a super geo is worth far more than a regular local market. ROI and lifetime value for one household is important, but not as relevant as ROI and lifetime value for a super geo, which better reflects the network effect of superconsumers and potential superconsumers in a particular super geo.

Superconsumers influence others in all kinds of categories. As I mentioned before, their influence works in private-label products. If I go to a friend's house and I see a lot of Kirkland-branded products from Costco, it has an impact on me. I start to think, "My friend is a smart guy. If private label is good enough for him, then maybe it should be for me as well."

In fact, part of Gladwell's quote very much explains the decade-long "overnight" success of Keurig. As Michelle Stacy, the former president of Keurig, told me, the super geo for Keurig was offices in New England. While the menu at Starbucks was growing rapidly for consumers, people working in offices were often stuck with the coffee that their office manager preferred. So the original Keurig founders targeted the $4 billion office-coffee market, which was dominated by Bunn and had lots of dissatisfied consumers. This dissatisfaction was critical to Keurig's entrance into the market, as the early Bunn machines cost $10,000 or so, something no individual consumer was going to pay for. Keurig consequently perfected its product, achieved scale, and reduced its costs, all by taking advantage of the displeasure of the office-coffee market.

In particular, the office market was the perfect marketing vehicle to enter the consumer market. Workers began to fax in pleas to buy a Keurig for their homes. But their demand was stoked not by a clever, high-cost marketing campaign. It was driven by paid sampling (paid for by the offices) and user experience. The Keurig phenomenon couldn't be explained; it had to be experienced. And as Gladwell says, it was better experienced among a group of coworkers who loved the product.

New England offices constituted the super geo for Keurig—the epicenter, if you will. It then spread to New England homes. And eventually, Stacy saw the product go from two million homes to sixteen million in six years.

As noted, super geos are not necessarily geographically defined. They are venues where superconsumers' passion can feed off one another in front of people who are not superconsumers. Technology has created great venues for superconsumers and other people to interact in the form of social media. My colleague Tim Joyce has done extensive work with top social-media companies. He has noted that crowdfunding businesses like Kickstarter have built their business models around superconsumers. Someone who is willing to fund a company to create a product that doesn't yet exist is by definition a superconsumer. Joyce has a friend who created Griz Coat. This Kickstarter-supported company makes the Griz Coat, a combined costume and coat—usually in the shape of a bear—that costs \$200. Only a superconsumer of—well, I'm not exactly sure— would be first in line to help bring this item to market.

And Griz Coat has continued to flourish, growing at an annual $1.2 million run-rate.[6]

Kickstarter understands, and depends on, the notion of superconsumers. Since its inception, more than 9.2 million consumers, or backers, have funded ninety thousand projects, to the tune of $1.87 billion. And Kickstarter has taken in nearly $100 million in helping to make these matches.[7]

HOW QUESTS AND SUPER GEOS CREATE CATEGORIES

Across the hundreds of companies I've worked with at the Cambridge Group, I've realized that growth strategies come in three flavors. The vast majority of growth strategies are predicated on stealing share by outspending, copying, or undercutting the competition. I call this approach *pie splitting* because the results don't last, and they often create hypercompetitive situations that shrink industry profit. A small minority seek to expand the category by increasing the number of consumers, the units per consumer, or the price per unit. My experience is that 80 percent of category growth is captured by 1 percent of the brands in the category, so category growth can be very successful as a strategy. But the ultimate growth strategy is to create a new category.

Successfully creating a new category requires that you remain the *category king*, a phrase coined by Chris Lochhead, Al Ramadan, Dave Peterson, and Kevin Maney, some friends in Silicon Valley. According to them, category kings are companies that "define, develop, and dominate new markets."[8] Lochhead, Ramadan, and Peterson run a category-design consultancy called Play Bigger Advisors. All are former entrepreneurs and operators who have founded, bought, sold, and run $1 billion technology companies. In one amazing study of five thousand IPOs, they discovered that category kings captured 76 percent of the market capitalization, even among some of the most successful companies.[9] We see the effects of these category leaders everywhere. Although Apple is one of the most successful category creators in history, it has rarely been the first right out of the gate—BlackBerry was first with the smartphone, and Rio had the first MP3 player.

Creating a new category successfully (e.g., remaining the category king) requires both breakthrough product innovation and breakthrough business-model innovation simultaneously. There are at least eight major levers across both types of innovation (figure 4-2). While it's not critical to innovate across all eight levers, it is important to innovate on both sides. In my research, companies that innovate only on the product side of figure 4-2 can perform well, but may not sustain their innovation over time or perform as well as they could.

My rule of thumb on breakthrough product innovation is that you don't have to literally create something entirely new to the world. It can be an idea borrowed from another part of the world but a concept that is new in your region. Your innovation doesn't have to be a new element on the periodic table, but can be a new product delivered at an exponential level of benefit at an exponentially higher

FIGURE 4-2

Eight major levels for creating a new marketing category

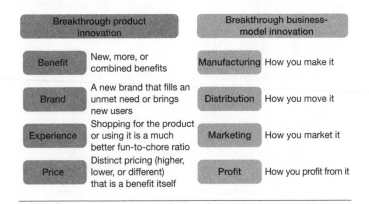

price point. Or it can offer a fractional level of bene-fit (previously unavailable) at a fractional and incredibly enticing price point (see, for example, the sidebar "Raising Prices"). Or it can be a combination of benefits in a new frame of reference at a combined price point.

Raising Prices

Rafi Mohammed, author of *The 1% Windfall* and *The Art of Pricing*, is my go-to strategist when it comes to pric-ing.* In his experience, which he outlines in his books and articles, even a 1 percent increase in pricing can drive a 20 percent increase in operating margins.

Mohammed's advice for better pricing—what he calls values-based pricing—is pretty simple: "Think like your customers." His four-step process, which I've out-lined below, is enhanced through superconsumers. Steve Clapp and Carl Gerlach, the former managers of Ball Park,

---

* Rafi Mohammed, *The 1% Windfall: How Successful Companies Use Price to Profit and Grow* (New York: Harper Collins, 2010); Rafi Mohammed, *The Art of Pricing: How to Find the Hidden Profits to Grow Your Business* (New York: Crown Business, 2005).

a popular hot dog brand, used a similar process to create a new premium product—angus beef hot dogs—that was priced higher than the company's other hot dogs.

Identify your consumer's next best alternative. Superconsumers suggested a much wider and interesting array of alternatives than did typical consumers: rather than listing other hot dogs or sausage as alternatives—which are obvious— superconsumers came up with McDonald's drive-through, beef jerky, rotisserie chicken, and protein shakes, among others.

Find out how your offer compares to the alternatives. While regular consumers would compare hot dogs with other hot dogs, superconsumers claimed that hot dogs weren't as fun as McDonald's and not as portable as beef jerky. They also had good things to say about the product: it's a perfect after-school snack because it's convenient, hot, and packed with protein.

Quantify the difference in dollars. Superconsumers had a much greater command of price points in the category. They knew that the next-best hot dog alternative to what was currently on the market was a kosher hot dog, which was $1.50 to $2.00 more expensive per package. So they were perfectly willing to pay $0.50 to $1.00 more for the angus beef hot dog because they believed it was still a great value.

Limit the incremental cost of goods. For angus beef hot dogs, the incremental increase in cost for the company was only a few cents per pound, but if the company had used resealable packaging to help consumers preserve their hot dogs, the cost would have increased by a lot. So the Ball Park marketers went back to their superconsumers, who were eating three or four hot dogs at a time. At this rate of consumption, the marketers figured that a resealable package was unnecessary. The lower price drove big profits, as customers flocked to the product because of its great value.

For breakthrough business model innovation, the threshold may not be as high as you think. Often, the innovation is a simple twist in changing a cost center into a profit center, much like how credit-card companies take their call centers and strategically use them to cross-sell new products.

Figure 4-3 shows how some well-known category creators have achieved their success. For all these companies, their success lay in some level of breakthrough innovation in both their offerings and their business models.

So how do you achieve breakthrough innovation in both the product and the business models? This is where the quest and super-geo ideas come in. Case in point is again American Girl.

My first trip to an American Girl store was overwhelming. The one in Chicago is in an upscale shopping building called Water Tower on the Magnificent Mile on Michigan Avenue. I often feel out of place in most luxury stores, but this place was so upscale, I ran out of the store briefly into a luxury fashion store simply because I needed to catch my breath. It reminded me of the first time I left Hawaii to come to Chicago. I felt like an alien on another planet.

Hundreds of superconsumer families (daughters, moms, aunts, grandmas), all on their own individual quests to learn, bond, and play, were densely packed into a beautiful retail store. I stood confused as superconsumers jostled past me. A doll hair salon? Truly Me Signature

FIGURE 4-3

Innovation matrix of category creation

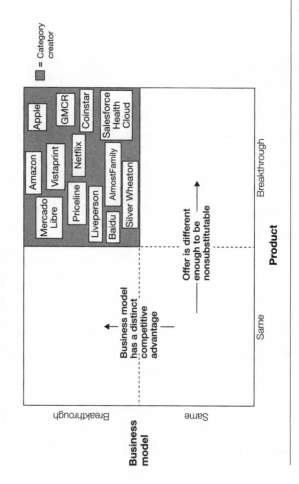

Studio? Hundreds of dolls stared me down. I would have felt less awkward wearing a Green Bay Packers jersey and a big cheese-wedge hat in the middle of a bunch of rabid Chicago Bears superfans at Soldier Field.

I had walked into an entirely new category that American Girl had created.

While dolls and accessories are not new per se, the combination of dolls plus accessories, educational multimedia, and a retail experience was a breakthrough product innovation. By aspiring to solve a broader quest of family intimacy and edutainment—and not just the job of a toy to play with or a book to educate—Mattel, which acquired the American Girl brand in 1998, has created a device-slash-consumable model (doll plus accessories and media) as powerful as Gillette's or Keurig's. In many respects, the merchandiser took Disney's model—movie to merchandise to experience—and resequenced it to merchandise to experience to movie.

This product and services ecosystem solved two major business problems that toy companies often face—uncertainty and SKU (stock-keeping unit) proliferation. Toy companies, not unlike fashion brands, don't really know what will be a big hit. For example, the success of the movie *Frozen*—and subsequent merchandising—was a big surprise for all. And since there is so much uncertainty, SKUs proliferate as companies try to spread their bets across multiple products. There's also the issue of volume. Since hit products are random, it's hard to predict how much product to make. And on top of that, given that multiple suppliers are required, the same product will sometimes have multiple UPCs (universal product codes), making data management a real challenge. American Girl avoids those headaches by releasing a limited number of historical characters—usually one per year. And the corresponding accessories and media make a historical doll much less seasonal than that of a typical hot toy.

Similarly, American Girl created a breakthrough business model with its retail stores, which serve as both a retailer and a sort of theme park. The theme park experiences, like the doll hair salon, a café for high tea, and the Truly Me Signature Studio (where you can customize flair for your doll), are huge traffic drivers. They also offer a reason to build stores with much more square footage than a typical toy store. The huge stores help distinguish American Girl dolls from other dolls, though the stores have a much smaller footprint than an actual theme park.

Finally, the dual nature of the retail-store-as-theme-park serves as a tremendous marketing vehicle. Although American Girl's marketing is spread across retail, direct-mail catalogs, and movies and books, the retail stores offer superconsumers a place to congregate into super geos. In terms of breakthrough business-model innovation, American Girl avoids the traditional toy route of national distribution and mass reach and instead taps into regional and local super geos.

LESSONS LEARNED

The success of American Girl offers us three lessons. All the lessons stress the importance of looking beyond everyday marketing issues and creatively listening to your superconsumers.

Superconsumers Beget Superconsumers

The true value of superconsumers lies in their contagious nature. Those you meet are likely to have a crowd of other current superconsumers and potential superconsumers with them. For additional superconsumers, look to their family and friends. Capture and share the superconsumers' stories, and watch as their knowledge inspires and creates new superconsumers.

Superconsumers Travel in Packs, Creating Super Geos

As the epicenter of demand creation, super geos can be tapped into to drive superior growth in your business. But you must locate and leverage them. The words *national average* are some of the most misleading in business. Many leaders have an inherent, subconscious belief that demand is spread like peanut butter, evenly and thinly. But the very presence of super geos means that passion for your offering will be patchy, with one set of consumers wild about your product while another group is neither hot nor cold. If you believe that demand is like the flat Midwest, then you'll be ill prepared to climb the hilly terrain it really is.

Superconsumers Are Superconsumers of Multiple Products

A superconsumer of one category is often a superconsumer of other categories. Cleverly combining two or more important, yet seemingly different categories not only taps into a quest, but can also create a new category—just as American Girl crashed dolls, education, and experiential retail into one category.

Generac, the leading manufacturer of standby generators, found that people who buy three to four times more life insurance and lots of vitamins tend to be great prospects for proactively buying a generator for an extreme event that may never happen. These consumers are superconsumers of proactive protection.

Sometimes the connection between categories is not as clear, as some categories counterbalance one another. For example, superconsumers of milk tend to be superconsumers not of other healthy foods and beverages, but of more indulgent ones like cereal, cookies, and candy. Milk was the perfect accompaniment to sweets—and was probably considered something like an old-school indulgence you could buy from the Catholic Church in advance of a sin you were planning to commit. Counterintuitively, *Harvard Business Review* reported that shoppers who recycle their grocery bags tended to indulge more in junk food as well.[10]

What Pleasant Rowland created and Mattel helped foster is amazing. American Girl's remarkable growth may also feel intimidating. But it is more feasible than you might think, especially considering how low the success rates are for innovation in your core business.

The key is to take stock of the state of your business now. Are you hitting your growth goals? How good is your ROI now? What are the odds that your business will still be successful for the next five to ten years?

Of all new consumer packaged goods, 85 percent or more fail.[11] Why? Often, the problem is that they aim too low by trying to solve the same job with a slightly modified product. Companies would do far better aspiring to solve a quest, but falling short slightly and finding that they created a product that consumers wanted to hire for a wholly more important job than its originally intended one.

The most successful businesses today have multiple business models, not just one. How well does a unidimensional business model do against a multidimensional one? Poorly, much like a boxer who runs up against a mixed martial artist who can box, kick, and wrestle. It is an unfair fight. This is both the beauty and the imperative of leveraging superconsumers to create new categories.

part three

HOW YOU CAN DO IT

chapter 5

BUILDING RELATIONSHIPS

Just about every company considers itself customer-centric if it uses focus groups, surveys, and ethnographies. But the truth is, very few firms develop deep relationships with their consumers. They don't seriously participate in a two-way dialogue, and they only reach out to consumers on their own terms, on their own turf, and on their own time. It is not a real relationship, because it is one-way and the companies can't feel real empathy for consumers.

Mark Cuban, an early internet billionaire and the owner of the Dallas Mavericks, has famously said, "You don't own your business. Your customers do." Given this observation, you don't need just to spend time with your customers. You need to build a friendship with them.

To be fair, it probably makes little sense to invest a lot in building a relationship with an average consumer who perhaps thinks of your category for a few seconds on the odd occasion. But superconsumers are different. Relationships with them can offer both very high ROI and personal rewards for the consumers as well.

WHY BUILDING FRIENDSHIPS IS IMPORTANT

Greg Gallagher, senior director of strategy for Crown Imports (distributor of Corona), helped me come up with a framework for building relationships with superconsumers for profitable growth. To summarize the four important steps of this approach, we label it the FUEL framework:

1. **Find superconsumers.** You have to find them three ways: (1) analytically in your data, (2) internally within your team, and (3) personally among your family and friends.

2. **Understand superconsumers.** There are four ways to understand them: (1) rationally, (2) emotionally, (3) contextually, and (4) culturally.

3. **Engage with superconsumers.** You engage with them in two ways: (1) by having empathy for the heights and depths, joy and pain, of their superconsumer passion and (2) by understanding your own role in contributing to their pain and joy.

4. **Lean into superconsumers.** Just as Sheryl Sandberg, in her book *Lean In*, encourages business to lean into the untapped potential of women, I am similarly encouraging business to lean into the untapped potential of superconsumers.[1] Sandberg's idea of a lean-in circle, where women get together regularly in small groups to learn and grow together, is similar to a super geo, where superconsumers cluster together. For superconsumers, it is not enough to give them a seat at your table. Make sure there are multiple seats for multiple superconsumers, and watch them riff off each other for new ideas for growth. Seek out how superconsumers have fun with your category. Understand the category's challenges

and chores. Look for bias, and shatter stereotypes of superconsumers. Look for ways that you can help your consumers a great deal but at low cost to yourself. Be generous. It's the only way to start a real friendship.

If you perform each step of this four-step process to the best of your ability, you should see an increase in revenue. Consider this equation:

$$revenue = A \times B \times C \times D$$

A is the number of markets, B is the number of consumers in a market, C is the number of units per customer, and D is the price per unit. Figure 5-1 shows how this equation

FIGURE 5-1

FUEL profitable growth through superconsumers: a revenue equation

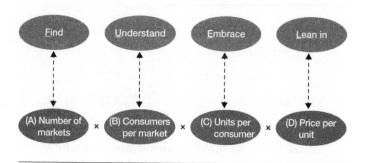

relates to the FUEL framework. Let's look at these relationships in detail:

Finding your superconsumers helps you with variable A (number of markets). Most large companies and brands believe that their business is truly national. The opposite is actually more accurate. The root cause of this misconception is the extremely popular metric of *national market share*—your business's or brand's percentage of total volume, sales, or profit for an entire country. National market share is one of the most misleading metrics out there.

Let's say brand X has a 20 percent national market share. This percentage sounds pretty good, with still some room to improve. The reality is that brand X's business is rarely 20 percent anywhere, but more like 30 percent or higher in some markets (really strong) and 10 percent or lower in other markets (much weaker). Brand X may be available everywhere in the country, and its marketing may reach everywhere in the country. But the brand would do better having two distinct strategies tailored to its strong and weak markets.

Conversely, up-and-coming brand Y might have a national market share in the low single digits. A big player might dismiss the brand as inconsequential. This viewpoint would be accurate if the share were in the low single digits everywhere. But brand Y has the second-largest market share in a few local markets. And if that 20 to 30 percent market share is enjoyed in trendy, forward-looking local markets, then watch out for brand Y's future.

Most businesses are hyperregional. Once companies understand that they are more regional than national, they realize they can often reallocate resources to improve their ROI.

Understanding superconsumers helps you with variable B (consumers per market). By learning about your superconsumers, you can gauge where consumers sit on the "making of a superconsumer" spectrum. Many companies assume that if consumers in a market are aware of their brand and have convenient access to it, their job is done. But these firms don't realize that some markets are better positioned for key life-stage triggers that often transform a normal consumer into a superconsumer. For example, college towns are a great place to reach consumers with new financial services like credit cards. And other markets are at the tipping point of becoming a super geo; their superconsumers are close together either physically or emotionally (through social media or other forms of communication). The closeness creates the exposure, education, and personal experience that accelerate growth.

Engaging superconsumers uses insights from variable C (units per consumer) to drive share of wallet. Superconsumers who buy five times more units than the average consumer does are not five times richer. Nor are their households five times bigger. But these superconsumers have discovered new jobs to be done for the category, and these jobs mount up into a broader life quest. Understanding how superconsumers view a product as part of this quest helps you identify which categories superconsumers are "firing" (dropping) to "hire" (purchase) more of your category. This knowledge is often the best inspiration for innovation and marketing.

Leaning into superconsumers helps unlock variable D (price per unit). Raising prices can be extremely lucrative, but it's usually not done well—or at all— because it seems risky. Companies tend to raise prices only when they are facing external pressure, like rising commodity costs or when a strong market leader raises its prices. The great thing about superconsumers is, they actually *want* you to raise the price, but in exchange for the right benefits. The easiest way to confirm that someone is a superconsumer is by asking the consumer, "What would need to be true for the price of this category to be twice as much as it is today?" An average consumer would be perplexed and likely be outraged at the very idea. A superconsumer will give you a long list of benefits they want and value, even at more than twice the present price. Your job is to simply figure out how to deliver the benefits they want at a price that is less than the value of the benefits but greater than the cost to do so.

With that in mind, let's dig deeper into each step of the FUEL framework.

FINDING SUPERCONSUMERS

As mentioned earlier, you can find your superconsumers in three ways—within your data, among your team, and among your family and friends.

Finding superconsumers through data is possible even if you think you don't have great data. Anyone can do this, even if you don't have direct relationships with consumers. You just have to look for the ripple effects and reverberations of superconsumers in the data you already have. Superconsumers are like powerful magnets that distort the data around them. They leave footprints and other telltale signs that they exist. Given that many leaders fail to recognize the importance of their super-consumers, most businesses are probably sitting on more data than they realize.

All businesses have local market data, whether it is numbers on customer relationship management, sales, or shipments. A market can be a region, a zip code, or even your block. What's more, variance exists in every data set. The key is to normalize it on a per-capita basis (and to control for local market factors) so that you can separate superficial variance from meaningful variance.

Once you've culled the superficial variance, you can begin asking a thousand whys about the root cause of the significant variance. Through this journey of questions, you'll begin to find your superconsumers.

One of the greatest source of variance is sales per capita per market. This statistic is extraordinarily valuable as a business insight as well as a revealing sign of where your superconsumers are. If you run a global business, you are very familiar with sales per capita. The statistic can vary quite a bit in very obvious ways. For example, beer per capita is much higher in the Czech Republic (156.9 liters per person), Ireland (131.1 liters per person), and Germany (115.8 liters per person) than in other countries recently surveyed by CNBC.[2] Given certain common assumptions about local culture and market nuances, these forerunners are probably not surprising to you.

But what if similarly high levels of variance per capita existed in the same country? Can you guess whether New Hampshire or Texas has the highest per-capita consumption of beer? You might be tempted to guess Texas, where everything is big. You might also think that Texas is the winner because its warmer climate might increase its population's thirst for beer. But New Hampshire, at 42.2 gallons per capita per year (according to the Beer

Marketing Institute), is higher than Texas, whose citizens drink 33.2 gallons of beer per capita per year.[3]

Why? Figure 5-2 might be illuminating. It shows that a much higher share of the national sales volume of beer goes to craft beer in the New England area, which New Hampshire is a part of. And since craft beer is a high-engagement sector and a more expensive one, New Hampshire rises above Texas.

Variance doesn't stop at the regional level. I have seen significant variance at the state, city, and even the zip-code levels. The key is to find the right level of granularity that

FIGURE 5-2

Craft beer, national versus regional share of volume

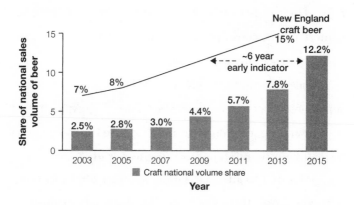

Source: National Brewing Association, Craft Brewing Business, and TCG analysis.

makes the most sense for your business. Business models that distribute via warehouses only need regional or state-level granularity, whereas direct-to-consumer businesses prefer an extremely granular view.

The second great way to find superconsumers through data is to use digital means—social media, mobile, and e-commerce. Ben McConnell outlined the 1 percent rule in social media ten years ago.[4] Based on an analysis of *Wikipedia* content, the rule established that 1 percent of users of social media generate the vast majority of content. They do so because they are the most passionate users out there. Given this observation, when anyone is creating content—a Facebook post, photos on Pinterest, videos on YouTube—about your category, the odds are extremely high that the person is a superconsumer. Average consumers might consume the content, but they are highly unlikely to actually contribute.

Mobile apps and e-commerce are also easy ways to find superconsumers right under your nose. The majority of your own time spent on your mobile device is dominated by a small handful of apps, according to a study Nielsen conducted for the Coca-Cola Retailing Research Council (figure 5-3). Similarly, the majority of your personal e-commerce spending probably goes to a few leading e-commerce companies like Amazon and Alibaba. Consequently, if you have a consumer who has taken the time to download your app or create a login, password, and profile on your e-commerce site, most likely he or she is a superconsumer.

FIGURE 5-3

Most-often-used smartphone apps

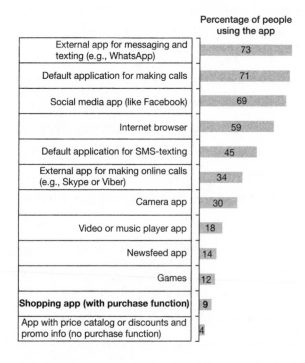

	Percentage of people using the app
External app for messaging and texting (e.g., WhatsApp)	73
Default application for making calls	71
Social media app (like Facebook)	69
Internet browser	59
Default application for SMS-texting	45
External app for making online calls (e.g., Skype or Viber)	34
Camera app	30
Video or music player app	18
Newsfeed app	14
Games	12
Shopping app (with purchase function)	9
App with price catalog or discounts and promo info (no purchase function)	4

Source: Nielsen, quantitative survey, conducted for Coca-Cola Retailing Research Council, Eurasia and Africa, first quarter 2016.

Once you have found superconsumers in your data and through apps and social media, you are ready to move on to the next step. But before you do that, it is important to look around you and see if you have superconsumers on your team and among your friends and family. This step is often overlooked, but it is extremely empowering, especially to your team members. Employees raise their level of engagement when they realize that the company they work for is serving a close friend or a family member in an area they really care about. These employees then start to talk with their personal superconsumer and will come back with insights about how to find more superconsumers in clever, nonlinear ways. For example, per the US Energy Information Administration, 23 percent of US households have two or more refrigerators.[5] That figure may seem only of interest to appliance manufacturers, but I found that households with multiple refrigerators stock and freeze much more food. Households with enough food stored are much more likely to buy standby generators. Generator buyers are much more likely to have more life insurance than they need. Those with more life insurance than they need are much more likely to be superconsumers of vitamins. The common unifying quest for these consumers is an inherent motivation exemplified by the Boy Scouts of America motto "Be Prepared." We will come back to this idea of superconsumers' begetting more superconsumers, but for now, consider the potential connections within your own groups of superconsumers, as these relationships will be extremely handy in your growth strategy.

UNDERSTANDING YOUR SUPERCONSUMERS

Understanding superconsumers may be the hardest step in the process, especially since you'll have to relate to them in four ways—rationally, emotionally, contextually, and culturally.

But before you can relate to people, it is important to keep a few things in mind:

1. People are different, and they value different things. Your worldview may not be the same as theirs.

2. People are logical. It is not obvious at first, but when you understand the context surrounding people's behavior, their actions often make complete sense.

3. People are emotional. People's emotions are powerful and primal, and we can only understand them through empathy.

Let's see how these three observations apply to the craft beer business, which has been growing nationally and even faster among leading markets and consumers. Keith Levy, the former vice president of marketing and sales for Anheuser-Busch, is now the US president of Royal Canin, a highly specialized, super-premium pet-food company and a division of Mars Inc. He shared his insights with me from his two decades in one of the most successful beer businesses in history.

Levy and his team were looking to create a new premium beer to accompany their line of Bud Light products. They were researching the market and interviewing superconsumers to get a firm grasp on what direction they should move.

The team knew that drinkers of alcoholic beverages value image—their own self-image and the image they want to project to others—more than taste, health, convenience, and price when making purchases. Look at it this way. You would never ask a person, "What kind of milk guy are you—organic? Skim?" It sounds silly.

However, swap out beer, wine, or spirits for milk, and it is a totally different story. Let's say you had to pick between two men to back you up in a fistfight. All you know about them is that one man likes to drink Wild Turkey bourbon, and the other likes white wine. Which fighting partner would you pick? I thought so! Is a man who likes to drink Wild Turkey definitely a tougher fighter than one who drinks white wine? No, but that is the image that we form in our minds. So we're all conscious of these images when we're buying alcohol, and it affects our decisions.

In prior research, Levy and his team had used a technique called *psychological drawings* to gather more insights about the image consciousness of consumers. Specifically, they asked participants to draw a picture of another person who loved expensive beer.

One man drew another man accompanied by two bikini-clad women on a beach. When asked to provide more context, he said the man in the picture was a twenty-seven-year-old talent agent who recently found success at work. He was six feet one, 180 pounds, and a smooth dresser. The women, he noted, were twenty-four and twenty-five. "He comes off as a young, good-looking success story . . . Others are automatically drawn to him," he said. The consumer who drew the picture did not necessarily resemble the man in the picture. But that was the image of the man he hoped to be.

This macho culture was changing, however, and the market was shifting toward sweeter flavors. Were brown spirits like scotch and other whiskeys—very strong, acquired tastes—growing? Yes, but not nearly as fast and big as flavored vodkas. Were hoppy India pale ale (IPA) craft beers growing? Yes, but not nearly as fast and big as Corona and a wide variety of wheat beers; consumers liked to add a slice of citrus to these beers to enjoy them. The challenge for Levy's team was to figure out why consumers were moving toward sweeter beverages.

As the team dug deeper and interviewed the super-consumers, it found that a meaningful number of them didn't enjoy the taste of beer. When asked how long they continued to drink their favorite beer until they acquired the taste, they answered "months." Such slowly acquired appreciation rarely occurs in food and other beverages, where consumers often choose taste above all. But in the case of beer, image—again—trumped taste (figure 5-4).

In fact, nearly 30 percent of consumers who regularly drank beer did not necessarily like its taste. Industry estimates put the overall US beer market at more than $100 billion annually.[6] This means that about $30 billion of

FIGURE 5-4

The broken compromise: using superconsumers to uncover which demand truly drives alcohol consumers

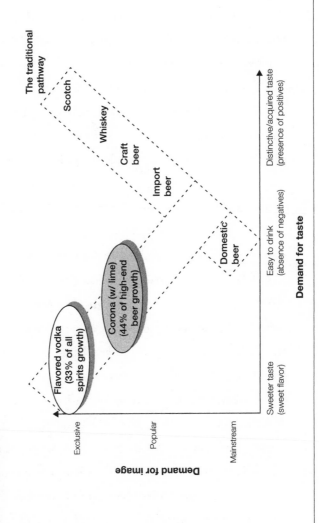

beer was either at risk—or constituted an opportunity—if this compromise between some consumers' dislike of the taste and their desire for a certain image could be broken.

Here is where Levy and his colleagues had a choice to make. They could go sweet or not go sweet. This wasn't an easy decision. On the one hand, considering beer's macho culture, it would have been easy to dismiss these consumers with sweet palates as people who did not know better. In fact, a year earlier, the industry ran commercials saying, "You just don't put fruit in your beer." But on the other hand, the numbers were clear: one-third of a beverage's market wasn't too wild about the beverage's taste.

Before marketers made a decision, they sought to learn more about why drinkers were moving toward the sweet end of the taste spectrum. They came up with a few reasons. The next generation of beer drinkers grew up in the world of coffee shops, which sold more milk than actual coffee (the average Starbucks drink has eighteen ounces of milk and two ounces of coffee), which meant that consumers had been cultivating sweeter palates for years.[7] The members of the team knew that vodka brands had been selling citrus and sweet-flavored varietals for years. They also saw that the wine and spirits market, which is 60 percent male and 40 percent female, was winning out over beer, which is 80 percent male and 20 percent female, and that women physiologically have sweeter palates than men do.

In the end, the team decided to engage with its superconsumers to guide its decisions. The group could have forgone this step and followed what it thought was the prevailing industry wisdom. Such an approach would have shown a certain level of contempt for the consumer—contempt that businesses often don't realize they have (see the sidebar "Calibrating Your Contempt for Your Consumers").

Calibrating Your Contempt for Your Consumers

If we're truly honest with ourselves, many business leaders have hidden levels of contempt for their consumers. Few leaders are openly hostile and contemptuous of their consumers, but many leaders have more contempt than they realize. In the same vein, too many companies believe they know better than their consumers do. How many companies have reduced the quality or size of a product but held the price the same because they believed that consumers wouldn't notice? Or which companies have made innovation decisions based on what they do well instead of what the consumer really wants?

The underlying, subtle contempt behind all of these decisions is that the company has more power than the consumer. "The consumer has no other choices, because the world revolves around our brand," goes the company thinking. "The consumer has no information, so we can sweep this under the rug if we want." Or, "The consumer has no voice; we are the ones with big media budgets." Certainly, hypercompetition—that is, perfect information on the internet that enables fast followers and frenemies (e.g., retail partners who replicate your product via private label)—has changed all of these things.

What you believe about your consumers shapes every business decision you make. Everything is affected, whether the decision is consumer oriented (e.g., a new product) or not (e.g., a new manufacturing process). In fact, businesses hold many kinds of consumer beliefs and follow the natural behaviors—and outcomes—these beliefs lead to.

Try the quiz in figure 5-5 to gauge your company's contempt level for its consumers. Answer the question on

FIGURE 5-1

Gauging your company's contempt level for its consumers

What you believe about consumers

1. Do you believe all consumers are the same?
   a. No
   b. Yes

2. Do you believe your consumers can spend more?
   a. Yes
   b. No

3. Do you believe your consumers are smart?
   a. Yes
   b. No

4. Do you believe your consumers are powerful?
   a. Yes
   b. No

5. Is your relationship with your consumers more . . .
   a. personal?
   b. transactional?

What your actions actually reveal

1. Are you investing more in . . .
   a. increasing and innovating your portfolio of offers?
   b. increasing scale and efficiency?

2. Do you focus on measuring . . . .
   a. tomorrow—lifetime value, loyalty?
   b. today—penetration, share, buy rate?

3. How much of your marketing is . . .
   a. consumers talking you up to other consumers?
   b. you talking at consumers about your business?

4. Is your approach to customer service . . .
   a. like a P&L—kill them with kindness?
   b. like a cost center—less people, less time, etc.?

5. Does more of your recent profit growth come from . . .
   a. investing more in products and raising prices?
   b. cutting back on your products, your prices, or both?

the left first, then the question on the right. There are two scores to calculate—the first score is how self-aware you are about your level of consumer contempt, and, the second, how much contempt you actually have.

Count how many times your answer on the left was the same letter as the corresponding answer on the right (i.e., you answered "a" on both sides). If you got a score of 4 or 5, then your actions match your beliefs. Anything below that, and either you are not self-aware or your organization is not aligned.

Second, count how many "b" answers you have for all ten questions. If your score is 0 to 3, then you have very little contempt for your consumers. For any score of 4 or above, you have a good amount of contempt for your consumers. Too much contempt represents a risk and an opportunity cost for your business.

If your company didn't fare well, don't worry. The key is to be self-aware and to try to steer your organization toward a more empathetic culture.

ENGAGING YOUR SUPERCONSUMERS

When they talk about engaging their consumers, many executives think it means a massive marketing campaign or a very expensive customer relations management effort. It doesn't have to be. It's likely that your superconsumers are already engaging with your company. You just have to interact with them.

The simplest way to engage with superconsumers is the same way you build personal relationships. This means you must listen and reflect, be curious and highly observant—and act generously, which is the lean-in part of the framework. Let's look at how Keith Levy and his team at Anheuser-Busch employed these practices.

Listening and Reflecting

To build engagement, you listen to superconsumers, then play back what you heard to fully understand. This is not the time to defend your company's decisions, solve problems, blame, argue, or make excuses. This took me a quite a while to learn.

Levy did an admirable job of listening and reflecting. From the data, he saw that consumers were no longer willing to compromise their palates for the image they wanted to project. He listened to them, and upon reflection, he accepted what they told him as fact. He also saw that with the growth of social media, consumers were using products from a host of categories to project their images and that beer might lose its place if Anheuser-Busch didn't move quickly.

Being Curious and Highly Observant

The next step is to ask more questions to understand why your consumers are acting the way they are. In Levy's case, he and his team had to determine why consumers were shifting to stylish and slightly sweet beers. They found that male consumers were making the shift when they began living with their girlfriends or wives. Since these consumers didn't have kids yet, they were still looking to socialize and have fun, but they also wanted a drink that they could share with their significant others. A slightly sweet and stylish beer did the trick.

LEANING IN

The last step is to give your superconsumers what they're asking for. Levy and his team, for example, created a new product, Bud Light Lime, an idea that they'd previously dismissed. But with the help of their superconsumers, they found a precise level of sweetness, they dropped their traditional brown bottle (no small decision) in favor of a clear bottle that signaled more style, and they changed the tone of their advertising in nonsports contexts to be more male and female. Finally, they elevated the packaging and price point, merchandising it away from Budweiser but closer to the other high-style, slightly sweet brands like Corona and Blue Moon. The last sticking point was what brand to put on it—Bud Light or a new brand?

Seeking Challenges and Taking Risks

The choice of brand was a hugely controversial and risky decision. Every senior executive at Anheuser-Busch had once been the Bud Light brand manager. Over the years, more than $1 billion of advertising had been invested to build the Bud Light brand, which was the largest brand in the world when Levy's team was deciding what to name this new beer. No one wanted to be the first to feminize the brand. Some argued that a new brand would not only be safer, but also be more appealing to consumers. In testing this concept, consumers loved the innovation right away. But they kept saying, "Isn't this just Bud Light with lime in it? Why not just keep it simple and call it that?" It turns out consumers were also worried about the risk of drinking something slightly sweet that did not convey the image they wanted. Consumers were really saying, "Give me a popular, mainstream brand like Bud Light to legitimize this."

So the marketers went for it. They took a chance with the biggest beer brand in the world. Not just because it was right for the consumer, but because the gap of what consumers really wanted in a slightly sweet yet stylish beer brand and what was available to buy was so big. And they moved very fast.

The traditional incubation period at Anheuser-Busch was eighteen to twenty-four months to fully develop an idea and bring it to market, but since Levy knew the opportunity was so rich and the need to move quickly was critical, he took smart shortcuts and launched Bud Light Lime in less than a year. It was one of the most successful new beer brands ever launched in the history of the beer industry; the superconsumers had paid back the company's efforts to listen to and understand them.

And this strategic move was the gift that kept on giving. Levy, Pat McGauley (vice president of innovation), Gregg Billmeyer (vice president of strategic initiatives), and Marlene Coulis (vice president of insights) created a mega-brand platform for the Bud Light brand. The platform included Bud Light Lime, then Bud Light Platinum, and, eventually, Bud Light Lime-A-Rita.

The last product was the key. Anheuser-Busch created a new category of beverages (not a beer, not a spirit, but something in between), which allowed the company to compete with spirits without writing big checks to buy its way into spirits. This innovation platform drove huge profitable growth for Anheuser-Busch (figure 5-6).

Acting Generously

Generosity can be a highly effective growth strategy.[8] Most business is viewed as zero-sum when it comes to competition—and too often when it comes to consumers. But occasionally, a company will recognize the benefits of generosity. Nordstrom's generous return policy and customer service has been highly effective. Costco is well known for its veritable free lunch buffet and samples. Gillette gives away free razors to teenagers for their first shave. How about even "discount brands" like Southwest and its bags-fly-free campaign?

Here's the singular theme that is common across these brands. They are all great products and experiences. And they know that giving you a little taste of something great will have you coming back for a lot more—at full price.

FIGURE 5-6

Bud Light mega strategy is working

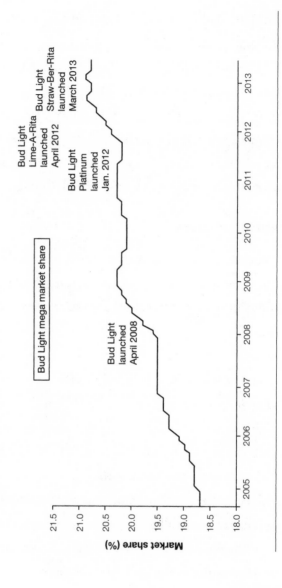

A more technical way of articulating this relationship is this: value comes from the benefits obtained for the price (value = benefits/price). When consumers see that the benefits of a product exceed its price for something they want, they sign up. The trick is to find benefits that people want and to deliver them in a way that your company's costs are less than the price you charge. Said another way, generosity can help you grow when value comes from the consumer's benefits, which are greater than the product's price, which is greater than your costs.

There are several ways to make the benefits exceed the price, to make the price exceed your costs, and to profitably grow your firm.

- **Offering things that make consumers feel great with low cost:** Commerce Bank (now TD Bank) found that free coin-changing machines drove new accounts. Consumers believed that this benefit meant the bank wouldn't nickel-and-dime them.

- **Seeing giveaways as high-impact, low-cost marketing:** A sampling study from Knowledge Networks PDI noted that sampling programs (the kind used at Costco) drove a 475 percent sales lift on the day of the event.[9]

- **Offering benefits in exchange for strategic information:** Most free-warranty programs are designed to gather detailed consumer information for purposes of customer relationship management.

- **Betting on lifetime value:** A single transaction might be a loss leader, but generosity has a big impact on loyalty and lifetime value. It's why Gillette offers free samples to customers at the age of eighteen and not thirty-eight.

As described earlier in the book, all of these generosity strategies are at play in Netflix's strategy and execution with *House of Cards*, a Netflix-original TV series. Releasing all thirteen episodes at once didn't increase the total production cost, but did make Netflix binge viewers very happy. This unusual release strategy generated a ton of buzz and goodwill among consumers. As CEO Reed Hastings noted, the big bang of releasing all thirteen episodes at once "reinforced our brand attribute of giving customers complete control over how and when they enjoy entertainment."[10]

The instantaneous release was a great way to quantify the emerging demand of binge-watching—something that Netflix's competition on regular TV can't easily accommodate. The move drove far more new subscribers with lots of goodwill than it did people trying to cheat the system. Netflix has always offered consumers a free one-month trial of its service, and one of the main concerns of Wall Street was that people would take advantage of the free-trial month and watch, say, all thirteen episodes of *House of Cards* and then quit. Netflix said that fewer than eight thousand free-trial subscribers actually did this, or about 0.6 percent of the 1.3 million people who signed on for the free trial in January.[11] Consumers tend to respond in kind when they are treated generously and with respect for something they value.

But the success of Netflix comes not just from its tactics, but also from how generosity flows throughout its brand and business model. In 2013, Netflix said that its subscribers watched four billion hours of media on Netflix across a total subscriber base of thirty-six million. According to Nielsen, the average person watches thirty-four hours of TV per week. That means Netflix subscribers watch about fifteen billion hours of total TV—broadcast, cable, and streaming TV—in a quarter. The latest numbers suggest Netflix accounted for approximately one-quarter of total TV viewing for its subscribers. But at $7.99 per month, Netflix only charges 10 percent of the cost of the average cable bill, which is around $80.[12]

If some skepticism remains about generosity as a growth strategy, then consider the alternative: stinginess as a growth strategy. Does that ever work in the long run? How does it work in the social era, where singular acts of generosity or stinginess spread like a virus? If Twitter is the TMZ, or Hollywood gossip page, for corporate behavior—good and bad—might generosity be the only viable choice in a digitally connected world?

Generosity may feel as if it is bad for business because it conjures up other words like *charitable* and *naive*. But the root word of *generosity* is closer to *ingenuity* and *ingenious*, both of which are very good for business. Generous companies appear to be proud of what they make. Panera is another example of a generous company. It knows that putting its great food in people's mouths—and letting those same people talk it up to others—is the best marketing for the restaurant. That's why Panera's donations-only cafés are breaking even, on average. Panera estimates that 60 percent of customers pay the suggested donation, 20 percent pay less (or nothing), and 20 percent pay more.[13] And Panera knows that generosity is highly empowering for employees and leads to wonderful stories (and PR).

Hastings recently reflected on the importance of generosity. In 2011, Netflix had tried to increase its rates and drop its DVD-mailing service at the same time. Thousands of emails from angry customers had poured in. "I realized," he said, "if our business is about making people happy, which it is, then I had made a mistake. The public shame didn't bother me. It was the private shame of having made a big mistake and hurt people's real love for Netflix that felt awful."[14]

Most CEOs don't talk about love very often. But by giving consumers benefits that feel generous, Netflix and other companies are creating long-term relationships with their superconsumers. And that is a highly effective way to grow.

chapter 6

INFLUENCING OTHER CONSUMERS

I've described in detail superconsumers and how superconsumer-centric companies have managed to make their best customers even better. And rightfully so. To make a superconsumer strategy work, you need to spend a lot of time, resources, and energy on understanding and innovating with this relatively small segment of consumers.

That doesn't mean that you should ignore the other 90 percent of consumers, however. They're important, too, perhaps more so. But like with many things in life, timing is everything. For many companies, you can be doing all the right things, but if you do it in the wrong sequence you may not get the full result you could. And once you build relationships with superconsumers, there are ways to use your newfound knowledge to influence three other groups of consumers that occupy different levels on the passion-and-profit index: potential superconsumers, autopilots, and uninvolved consumers (figure 6-1).

Potential superconsumers are the most intriguing members of the group. I've mentioned this segment before, specifically in the American Girl discussion, but it's worth revisiting them. These consumers are interested

FIGURE 6-1

Categories of consumers*

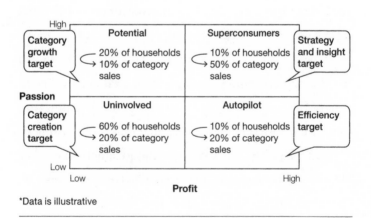

*Data is illustrative

and sometimes passionate about a category, but don't spend a lot—yet. Although they're usually younger and less well-off than superconsumers, their unwillingness to spend is more often attributable to a lack of education about a category and to fear. Because of their passion, however, they're the easiest to influence.

Autopilots spend a lot of money on a category but aren't very passionate. They're just going through the motions. This might seem counterintuitive, but many of us are autopilots in a variety of categories because of particular circumstances we find ourselves in or life stages we've entered into (e.g., getting married, having children). For example, since I travel frequently for work, I am an autopilot when it comes to taxis. But I do not find inherent joy in the taxi category.

Uninvolved consumers, who make up about 60 percent of consumers, are the largest group. Unfortunately, they act exactly as their name implies. They spend little, and they aren't passionate. Because of these tendencies, they're extremely hard to influence with business-as-usual methods. But these consumers can be swayed if you are willing to reinvent both the product or service and the business model. The video game category is a great example. When I mention video games, most people think of teenage boys playing violent or sports games on a game console in a dark basement. But from 2008 to 2011, the number of gamers doubled from 56 million to 135 million.[1] Much of this growth was driven by casual gamers playing free or cheap mobile and smartphone games like *Clash of Clans*, *Angry Birds*, or *Plants vs. Zombies*. With the reinvention of the experience (mobile versus console), the tenor (cute versus violent), and the pricing model (free versus costly, and everything in between), many of these new gamers are both younger and older than teen boys, and far more are female, including middle-aged and older women. Remarkably, mobile gaming overtook console gaming in 2015, with $37 billion in revenue versus $29 billion from console games.[2]

Since each segment of consumers is unique and reacts differently to advertising, pricing, and promotions, it can be very difficult—if not impossible—to create a strategy that appeals to everyone. A good strategy means that you can't do everything and serve everyone. But if you start with superconsumers, you'll have a better idea of how to engage with other segments and how many resources to devote to each group, depending on what your goals are.

THE FUN-TO-CHORE RATIO

To consumers, every category represents varying levels of fun and chores. If they find a category to be more fun than burdensome, then they tend to be more engaged and spend more. If they think a category is more of a hassle than a pleasure, they tend to be less engaged and buy less. You can see the fun-to-chore ratio in action at a place like Disney World.

I went to Disney World for the first time with my wife, our three kids, and several extended family members as reinforcements. I couldn't believe how exhausted I was, despite there being twice as many adults as kids. Waiting in line, keeping track of my kids, meeting Disney characters, about half of whom I had no real familiarity with: I had little fun with lots of chores. I was an uninvolved consumer.

Nevertheless, I was amazed by the Disney superconsumers at the park. They go out in the morning, then rest. Then they go out in the afternoon, then rest. Then they go back after dinner. They were so much smarter than I was about how to enjoy the theme park. They also seemed chipper.

I saw autopilots as well—often spouses married to Disney superconsumers. They enjoyed the experience, but not enough to make them forget how exhausting it was. And after our trip, I recognized many potential superconsumers. These are people who loved Disney when they were kids, but who have no kids of their own. They want to partake in the fun but don't want to go by themselves. So Disney is high up on their to-do list, right after giving birth.

By using superconsumers as your baseline, you can then take that knowledge and improve your product's fun-to-chore ratio to appeal to other consumers as well. To bring the potential superconsumers into the fold, you can make your products and customer experience more fun. To entice the autopilots, you can ask superconsumers how to reduce the biggest chores in your category and apply those insights. To unlock the latent demand of the uninvolved, you can reinvent the fun-to-chore ratio.

A great example of changing this ratio is Disney's MyMagic+ and FastPass system. This innovative system is tied into a radiofrequency identification (RFID) wristband. By signing up for the system, you can reserve your place in a ride line, pay for food, and even open your hotel door with the wristband. MyMagic+ and FastPass were perfect for Disney superconsumers who loved to enjoy their favorite rides repeatedly and get the most out of the parks. But the system was 87,000 percent more expensive than the $0.04 paper tickets Disney had historically used.[3] In 2011, the Disney board authorized $1 billion to invest in this new technology. Twenty-eight thousand hotel door locks needed to be replaced, and 30 million feet of Wi-Fi coverage needed to be installed.

But when the MyMagic+ and FastPass system was launched in 2014, it had a dramatic impact. Turnstile times were reduced by 30 percent. At the Magic Kingdom, the system has allowed more than five thousand additional people to enjoy the park at the same time. Over ten million people have worn the wristband and have been overwhelmingly satisfied with it.

Even for me, an uninvolved consumer for Disney parks, the new system makes me far more willing to go to Disney again! But remember the importance of timing and sequence. MyMagic+ and FastPass were designed with superconsumers in mind. If you had asked me—an uninvolved consumer—what the parks should have done, I would have told you to reduce the price and accept fewer guests so that the place would be less busy. And I'm sure I would have said, "Heck no, you can't put my credit card info on an RFID wristband!"

Let's now look at each segment of consumers in more detail.

POTENTIAL SUPERCONSUMERS

In my experience, potential superconsumers are the clearest sign of emerging and latent demand. Since they are passionate, they *want* to buy more products, but their lack of knowledge is holding them back. They just need to be encouraged. Potential superconsumers are open to letting you educate them, alleviate their fears, and convince them of the benefits and joys of a category.

Take wine, for example. Potential superconsumers want to be knowledgeable about wine and the differences between regions and blends. They want to learn how to choose a perfect bottle for dinner and one for different scenarios and seasons. The problem is that they lack the knowledge and experience to jump right in. Their hesitation isn't surprising, since wine can be a daunting category.

Now, imagine you're an executive in the wine industry. If these potential superconsumers (spending at a 50 index, that is, spending at half the rate of the average wine consumer) could become even a little bit like superconsumers (who spend at a 500 index, namely, five times the rate of the average consumer), there would be huge growth potential. If the potential group became a 100 index, the category would grow by 10 percent. If the group became a 150 index, the category would grow by 20 percent. And given that our research shows that 80 percent of category growth is captured by 1 percent of the brands, the growth would double and triple the value of a brand, respectively.

A good place to start is through more superconsumer-friendly marketing that celebrates and appreciates their love, cleverness, and knowledge, and then making sure that the marketing appeals to potential superconsumers as well. In other words, build the creative message with superconsumers, and test it with potential superconsumers. Often, brands buy their media to reach the most people in the most cost-efficient way possible. Thanks to advancements in big data and analytics, you can now maximize your reach to superconsumers and potential superconsumers first and then maximize your reach to other consumers. One of my clients described it as setting up your advertising as an engaging and fun conversation between two superconsumers, but allowing potential superconsumers and others to listen in.

Don Johnson, a fellow partner at the Cambridge Group, gives this example. Imagine you have a big product launch—say, a major DVD compilation of hip-hop music and history—and you are planning a big advertising push during either the Super Bowl or the hit TV show *Empire*. The Super Bowl would reach 112 million people, and a 30-second ad would cost $5 million. *Empire*'s viewership is about 10 million people, and a 30-second ad costs $600,000 toward the end of season one.[4] So the Super Bowl seems to make more sense—spend ten times more per ad, and get eleven times more audience. But as Johnson told me, "*Empire* is a brilliant combination of hip-hop music and culture, celebrities making cameos, and sure-thing soap-opera plot lines run by celebrated African American show-runner Shonda Rhimes. The show is not just appealing to African Americans, but also attracts consumers of all ethnicities who love African American culture." In fact, he notes, the season one finale had 21 million viewers, but drew more African Americans in absolute number than the Super Bowl did. Factor in other consumers who love African American culture, and you hit both superconsumers and potential superconsumers for a fraction of the price. Thankfully, big-data tools like Nielsen Catalina Solutions (which matches sixty million loyalty cards from grocery stores with the Nielsen TV panel) allow this to happen at great levels of precision.

Also, if you can identify certain trends that are emerging among your superconsumers, you will be in a better position to influence potential superconsumers. For example, figure 6-2 shows the sales of champagne over a twelve-month period. Not surprisingly, total category champagne sales peaked during the winter holiday season; sales were twice as high as they were in the summer months. But interestingly, sales to superconsumers in the winter months are about the same as in the summer months. Why are superconsumers buying champagne consistently year-round? Do they not celebrate the holidays? Or do they celebrate with something besides champagne?

The answer is, superconsumers do celebrate the holidays, and they do so with champagne. Just like other

FIGURE 6-2

Champagne sales over twelve months

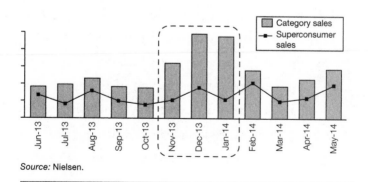

Source: Nielsen.

consumers, they "hire" champagne for the job of celebrating the holidays with others. The other answer is that superconsumers are also hiring champagne for an entirely different job in the summer—a job that, if other consumers knew how champagne could be hired successfully for a summer job, they might jump on board with, too! Why? The champagne superconsumers, who are mostly women, consider champagne a cool and refreshing alternative to beer, especially during hot outdoor barbecues. The problem, of course, is that champagne usually comes in large bottles—which is great for celebrations but not ideal if you want to enjoy a glass or two.

This observation led to an interesting opportunity for innovation: single-serve bottles of bubbly. As it turns out, single serve has become a growing trend with brands like Copa Di Vino, a premium wine-by-the glass company.

Superconsumers were happy with single-serve bottles, and so were potential superconsumers, who didn't have to commit to buying and wasting an entire bottle of champagne. And the single-serve bottles were more fun—consumers could try multiple varieties at minimal cost—which is usually a surefire way to make potential superconsumers more willing to buy more.

AUTOPILOTS

Frankly, it is very difficult to market to, innovate for, and sell to autopilots and expect them to change their behavior. Sometimes, even a lower price won't change their behavior, as the lower price may not be enough to warrant the inconvenience of changing their habits.

Still, autopilots provide several specific business opportunities around pricing innovation (e.g., subscription models) and so-called convenience innovation. Every category has burdensome chore elements that consumers have learned to live with because they assume these things can't be changed. Superconsumers are usually very vocal about these. The key is to listen and, if you need to, to make any adjustments that will improve their experiences. If you do so, autopilots may appreciate the efforts as well.

Two companies that have worked to reduce chores in their respective categories are Uber and Amazon. Uber has taken the chore out of getting a taxi. Through its app, consumers no longer worry about finding an available ride, paying for the service in cash, and providing feedback—good or bad—via tipping. The service is also cheaper than a taxi. In the future, as Uber becomes more ubiquitous, the price advantage will probably decline and the benefit will simply be convenience. Similarly, Amazon has lessened the chore of shopping by offering a huge assortment of goods at your fingertips, providing an easy way to research a product through reviews, and taking the friction out of the buying process through subscriptions and free shipping. Neither Uber nor Amazon is likely to grow their categories solely through chore reduction, but it certainly helps.

UNINVOLVED

The segment that generates the most discussion is the uninvolved consumer, because this group represents the biggest number of consumers and is too tantalizing for most companies to ignore. But to be honest, it is extraordinarily hard to influence a consumer who doesn't buy, care, or think that much about a category.

So how can you unlock the latent demand of the uninvolved? Start with superconsumers, and figure out a way to both increase the fun for potential consumers and decrease the chore for autopilots. Specifically, you have to dramatically change the fun-to-chore ratio with significant innovation on both the product side and the business-model side. In other words, you have to create a new category—a process employed successfully by American Girl (see chapter 4).

Let's go back to wine to look further at the potential in uninvolved consumers. I am an uninvolved wine consumer. Growing up in an immigrant Korean family in Hawaii, I didn't have wine on my radar screen. I rarely buy wine for myself, because I find wine intimidating and risky. But Fred Levy is a superconsumer of wine. He finds wine welcoming and a wonderful place to explore. Levy is originally from France, where wine was very much part of his cultural context. He is also the CEO of Coravin, a company with a product that serves both superconsumers and uninvolved consumers.

Coravin is a wine-serving product based on medical-device technology. The gadget enables consumers to extract wine by the glass from a bottle through a needle without removing the cork, thus preserving the remaining wine in the bottle. It's a remarkable product that brings the single-serve revolution to wine. My wife and I like it because it reduces the commitment of opening a bottle.

With its appeal to superconsumers like Levy and novices like me, Coravin has the potential to dramatically grow the wine category. My colleague Lindsey Leikhim and I estimate that the single-serve revolution could expand the category by several billion dollars (figure 6-3).

Coravin is a game changer because it enables consumers to experience wine in new ways. It also eliminates waste for couples whose preferences in wine differ. The ability to take a small glass of wine without opening a bottle is a big deal for novices like me. For example, people can throw dinner parties with ten-plus bottles of wine, allowing novices to try little samples of many wines to figure out what they really enjoy. Coravin can dramatically shrink the time it takes you to learn about the category and decide if you want to pursue it.

FIGURE 6-3

Superconsumers in the wine category

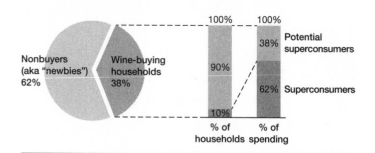

When I see Coravin at restaurants, I always ask the restaurant about it. Anecdotally, the restaurants I've spoken to are selling expensive wines four to six times faster. Few people might spend $200 on a bottle of wine at a restaurant, but more people might be willing to pay $75 for a single glass. We've also seen Coravin prominently used in a variety of establishments, from US restaurants like Morton's the Steakhouse to French wineries in Saint-Émilion, in the Bordeaux region. Target, Starbucks, and Whole Foods have already taken strides to shake up the model by elevating the in-store experience with wine service. Coravin could be the enabling technology to allow each shopper to have a glass of wine in-store while adding significant value to the retailers' bottom line.

The single-serve experience is a powerful intersection of great business economics (higher margins, incremental sales) and increased consumer benefits (more choice, more customization). Academics like Brian Wansink—a professor whose work helped create the 100-calorie snack pack—have written about this for years. Yet few companies have truly have made single serve accessible in the right way for consumers.

Other companies have found ways to increase fun while decreasing the sense of chores around a product as well. Keurig, for example, provides more than three hundred varieties of K-Cups (fun) that coffee drinkers can enjoy with simple push of a button without having to deal with waste or cleanup (no chores). The Keurig proposition so reinvented the fun-to-chore ratio of coffee at home, many people who don't even drink coffee own a Keurig machine, just so they can provide their guests coffee without having to worry about having fresh coffee in stock.

Even among Silicon Valley's best, the companies that have increased fun and decreased the sense of chore have enjoyed the highest valuations and the fastest velocity to market capitalization, as Al Ramadan, Dave Peterson, Chris Lochhead, and Kevin Maney, the authors of *Play Bigger*, have found (figure 6-4). And this success is largely because the companies achieved huge scale by hitting superconsumers, potential superconsumers, autopilots, and, most important, the uninvolved.

Let's go back to video games. As mentioned, no consumer category lacks superconsumers. However, no category has enjoyed such an extreme superconsumer effect as video games have. As described earlier, the growth

FIGURE 6-4

Top fifty consumer tech firms with fastest time to market capitalization

Consumer strategy	Example companies	Average valuation	Average velocity (market capitalization per year)*
More fun	Oculus, Pinterest, YouTube	$2 billion	$0.4 billion
Less chore	Nest, Uber, LinkedIn	$5 billion	$0.6 billion
More fun and less chore	Facebook, WhatsApp, Snapchat	$12 billion	$2.1 billion

*Excluding Facebook.
Source: Play Bigger "Time to Market Capitalization" report.

of video games has been driven by smartphone and other mobile games, of which many are casual games. The free games are supported by advertising, but the "freemium" category is driven by in-app purchases. Users can pay to upgrade their gear, to buy an extra life, or to buy anything else to enhance the gaming experience. Within casual games, 0.15 percent of gamers account for 50 percent of in-app purchase sales.[5] That is not a typo. If there were 10,000 gamers playing a game, only 15 of those gamers drove half the sales. The remaining 9,985 gamers enjoyed the game for free.

Is this distribution sustainable? No, it is not. But consider how this might be growing the total pie of gaming. The demographic breakdown of a traditional, console-based game like *Call of Duty* is 92 percent male, with the majority being under the age of thirty-five. A game like *Bejeweled Blitz*—a casual game—is 78 percent female, with the majority being between the ages of twenty-five and forty-four, and with a healthy spike of women over fifty-five.[6] Imagine if you could double the consumer base by simply creating games that a large, important demographic group—women and older consumers—might enjoy. Imagine if you could spread your cost structure of developers across a much wider population that is willing to pay a few dollars per game. Imagine a newly engaged thirty-five-year-old man trying to convince his fiancée— who couldn't care less about video games—that adding the latest $300 video game console to their wedding registry was a good idea. Now imagine that same man pitching his idea while his fiancée is fixated on her phone going for a high score on *Bejeweled Blitz*. The second scenario has much higher odds of success.

The influence of superconsumers on potential consumers is a common phenomenon. Think of your favorite hobby—something you spend a lot of time and money on and are really into. Did your hobby emerge out of thin air? Or did someone—probably a superconsumer—influence you with their infectious enthusiasm? Have you yourself ever influenced anyone to join in your interests?

Superconsumers influencing others is how demand spreads. And the spread of demand is how the total pie of any category gets bigger.

chapter 7

FINDING OPPORTUNITIES AND ALIGNING YOUR ORGANIZATION

As we've seen with the three case studies and other examples throughout the book, many aspects of business-to-consumer industries (B2C) are speeding up, which makes superconsumers all the more useful and powerful. New business models are transforming multiserve categories into single serve (e.g., coffee, wine, laundry detergent) and unlocking growth by increasing the price per unit. Venture-capital money is pouring into companies that are reinventing traditional products such as egg-less mayonnaise. There is likely to be more change in the B2C industry in the next five years than there was in the last fifty years.

This transition is not going to be easy—especially if you work for a big consumer company that is used to moving slowly and methodically. In the past, executives could sleep well without worrying that a new and relatively unknown company was going to disrupt the business the way that Netflix did to Blockbuster. This much certainty made strategic planning fairly predictable. Long-range plans that looked three years or further into the future were a relevant exercise. Annual operating plans could be developed eighteen to twenty-four months ahead. Retail resets could be done twice a year—in the spring and fall—like clockwork. Most media could be bought up front, months in advance. And it was more than OK to plan for, design, and perfect an innovation over the course of years before launching.

BUILDING AN EARLY-WARNING SYSTEM WITH BIG DATA

Big companies don't have the edge that they used to. As I noted earlier in chapter 3, in 2015, the twenty-five largest food and beverage companies were 45 percent of the category in the United States but generated only 3 percent of the total category growth and grew at 0.1 percent CAGR. Private-label goods drove 23 percent of the growth ($8 billion) and grew at 2.6 percent CAGR. But here's the shocking thing. Twenty thousand companies, none of which were in the top hundred, drove 49 percent of all category growth ($17 billion), growing at a 6.3 percent CAGR.[1] What do these companies have in common? They're small, and they can play fast.

While big B2C companies do try to be more nimble and agile, it is fundamentally futile for them to try to be faster than a small company. But big companies do have a true advantage over smaller ones: big data. Big data that incorporates superconsumers and super geos can serve as a trustworthy early-warning system that alerts you to opportunities that companies may have missed or ignored.

Figure 7-1 is based on the chart in chapter 5 that shows the surge in craft beer. If a beer company had noticed this trend, say, in 2011, it would have had a three- to four-year head start on some of its competitors. But if it had looked at superconsumers, too, who were driving craft beer sales way back in 2006, the company would have been ten years ahead of the current trend.

FIGURE 7-1

Surge in craft beer

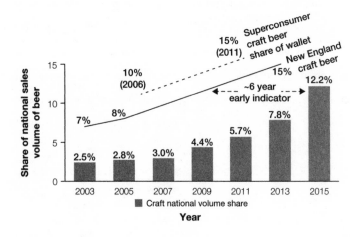

Source: TCG analysis.

Of course, you might be tempted to dismiss this chart as having the benefit of hindsight. But ask any leader who has been disrupted. Very few of them could say they never saw the disruption coming. No doubt, executives in the US yogurt business were aware of Greek yogurt and brands like Chobani and Fage. But disruptions are almost always underestimated or dismissed.

With the help of superconsumers and super geos, you can separate the real opportunities from the false ones. The beauty of this early-warning system is that it does not require a huge systems implementation that costs nine figures over multiple years. You're probably sitting on this data already. You just need to view it with superconsumers and super geos in mind (figure 7-2).

The point isn't to predict exactly when an opportunity will emerge. But you need to anticipate it far enough in advance so that you can start planning, act accordingly, and change your strategy as needed. Companies should no longer have one annual plan and one long-range plan. They should have different plans based on possible

FIGURE 7-2

Questions addressed by an early warning system

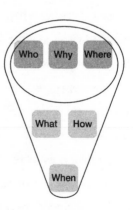

Who, why, and where?

- Who are the leading consumers?
- Why do consumers "hire" new or "fire" old categories?
- Where are markets leading, and where are they lagging?

What and how?

- What are the underlying features and benefits causing changes?
- How is this change spreading? What are the optimal conditions?

When?

- What is the rate of change in leading markets and in new markets?
- When is the tipping point for key decisions?
- What dashboards can be created on existing data?

opportunities—and threats. These trigger events and tracking systems should be in place already.

Here's an example of an early-warning system and the multitude of opportunities—and threats—that it could highlight. When I went to the beach as a kid in Hawaii, my family and friends were very religious about putting on sunblock. I remember regular warnings about melanoma as well as the shame you felt if you were a local who got sunburned. Usually, only tourists did not know better to protect themselves and got sunburned.

Shortly after I was married, I remember buying a rash guard for my wife. A rash guard is a cross between a very thin wet suit and a T-shirt. It was originally used by surfers and body boarders to prevent skin rashes from the friction between their stomachs and their boards as they paddled around. But fifteen years ago, when I got married, I remember seeing rash guards more regularly worn by nonsurfers, who valued the incremental benefits of warmth, modesty, and, most importantly, protection from the sun. The shirts have eliminated the hassle of putting on sunblock as well. Every year that we went to Hawaii, we'd see more people wearing rash guards. The shirts have grown to the point where almost every local I know wears one.

Each year, I would compare the near ubiquity of rash guards in Hawaii with their rarity in Chicago during the summer at the pool or the beach. It hadn't caught on yet. That rash guards will become mainstream is undoubtedly only a matter of time, where a small minority of consumers on the mainland at the beach will wear one. I am convinced of this when you consider the original benefits of a rash guard:

1. **Warmth:** Besides Hawaii, there are many other beach or lake cultures in the United States, and these are in colder climates than Hawaii. A water-friendly garment that provides warmth will only grow in demand.

2. **Modesty:** The rise of the selfie culture, coupled with the continuing rise of obesity, will only increase the level of self-consciousness consumers will feel in a bathing suit. Rash guards provide modesty that many consumers will want.

3. **Sun protection and avoidance of sunblock:** Today's rash guards have 50 SPF (sun protection factor), which is higher than some sunblocks. But more importantly, sunblock is a necessary evil and more

hassle than inherent joy. Most consumers find it
much easier to put on a rash guard than to apply
and remember to reapply sunblock.

This growing awareness of the benefits of rash guards
will create huge opportunities for apparel companies like
Under Armour, Nike, and Lululemon to move into more
premium-priced, functional clothing. It will also be very
disruptive to the skin-care category. Many skin-care and
sunblock companies have already innovated body-part-
specific sun protection, like a special lotion for the face, at
a high premium. These brands will find more growth, in
spite of the growth of rash guards. But sunblock brands in
the middle price range will likely have a very hard time
going forward, as the need to apply sunblock to the torso
diminishes with rash guards.

The key is to watch how quickly the rash guard spreads
beyond the super geo of Hawaii to other markets. Companies
have to watch markets that not only have a significant beach
culture, but that also consider fashion and looks a big deal—
like Los Angeles and New York. The trend has already
started to happen. Meaghan O'Connell celebrates the shirt
in a recent *New York Magazine* article: "I always thought of
bathing suits as a punishment for having a body, especially
an unruly one. *You can try to hide the rest of the year, but*

come spring break, the truth will come out . . . In my fashion rash guard, I feel protected from the sun but also sleek and vaguely athletic, like a seal who plays beach volleyball. Like, sure there is no way in hell I'm going to go parasailing today, but I *could*, you know?"[2]

Let's assume the first wave of rash guards occurred anywhere surfing culture already existed—places like Hawaii, California, and spots along the southeastern coast of the United States. Let's say the second wave is happening in nonsurfer, but high-fashion markets like New York or in summer lake cultures, like Seattle and parts of the Midwest. Or maybe it's happening in spring break destinations like Texas. Figure 7-3 shows how rash guard demand could spread organically. The next question is what an apparel company might do to take advantage of this spreading demand. The company could tailor the rash guard for different water activities, say, for more warmth for the boat and jet ski crowd, whose activities, especially in cold lakes, might call for a warmer garment. Another approach would be the fashion angle, in which a company could license brands like popular local colleges and schools.

Sun-care companies also benefit from an early-warning system when they take the growth of rash guards into consideration. They could anticipate where sales of rash guards have not yet hit big and place greater efforts there.

FIGURE 7-3

Hypothetical trigger event and tracking

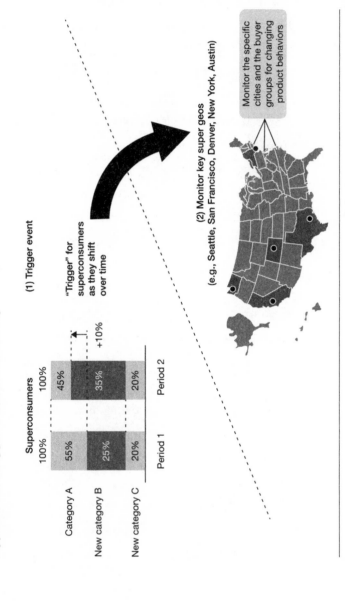

They could bet on innovations of sun-care products designed for parts of the body that rash guards will not cover, like the backs of hands, the back of the neck, and the face.

A precise early-warning system should excite or concern every function in your organization because it gives the functions specificity. Recognizing a future opportunity or threat is not just theoretical, but practical. When you use big data to build an early-warning system, the information you obtain becomes specific enough to take action on.

The scenarios should not be immediately jumped into, but rather lead to test-and-learn approaches in local markets (figure 7-4). That way, the very best data—actual in-market results—can guide your path.

FIGURE 7-4

Example of early-adopter and leading-indicator cities

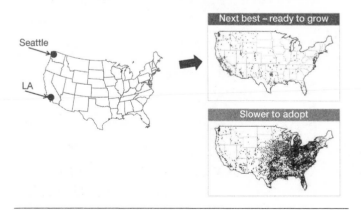

Once you have an early-warning system and precision map of how demand will evolve, make sure when making a business decision about superconsumers, you ask three questions:

1. Do superconsumers care? Will our offering help them achieve their quest and get their job done?

2. How much do superconsumers care? Will our offering make them want to use the category or pay twice as much, or do both?

3. Is how much they care greater than the incremental price they will pay, and is that price greater than my cost to deliver?

If you can confidently answer yes to all three questions, then you should feel empowered to move forward.

GETTING EVERYONE ELSE INVOLVED

As you begin to "superconsumerize" your data and use it as a warning system for various threats and opportunities, your intuition should improve over time. Eventually, you'll be able to quickly and easily discern which direction you should move in. And as you fine-tune and correct your superconsumer compass, you'll be in a better position to empower the members of your team and other colleagues throughout your organization to do the same.

Getting others on board is extremely important. From my experience, one of the best benefits of a superconsumer strategy is how the strategy makes it easier for cross-functional groups to rally around one common goal. But it also takes work to get everyone on the same page. You can do this by sharing superconsumer data with important stakeholders and involving them in discussions about the profitability of your category and the passion of consumers who buy your products and the products and your competitors.

As I mentioned in chapter 1, the beauty of superconsumers is that they're easy to understand. If you can show that 10 percent of your consumers are driving 50 percent of your profits, or even more, everyone's ears should perk up—especially those of the CFO. And especially if you can prove it with powerful data.

The best data is single-source data—purchasing behaviors and habits of individual superconsumers—since it will clearly show that the core essence of superconsumers is the magic that happens at the intersection of economics and emotion. These numbers should be loud and clear.

Most companies have reasonably good data to build a robust fact base on consumer profitability. Within the group of high-profit consumers, you need a simple, repeatable way to home in on those with high passion, too. This requires a few steps:

1. **Dream of a 360-degree data set.** Start with your data on consumer profitability, and imagine all the possibilities of data integration. What can the profitability data tell you about consumer behavior and emotions? Which other data sets can you link this data to, even beyond your category? Make a list of all the other data on behavior and emotion—both in and out of your category—that you can link your profitability data to. Breadth is more important than depth. Can you build a smaller subset of data that applies to superconsumers and that has much greater integration with other data sets (e.g., linking local sales to local social-media insights, linking credit card transactions and retail stores to build a unified view of the consumer, etc.)? When it comes to discerning passion, knowing how people spend

their time is as valuable as knowing how they spend their money.

2. **Identify predictors of passion.** Spend time with superconsumers both in the wild and within the four walls of your company. Some of the information that superconsumers will provide is incredibly powerful; that is, even a small amount of this data can predict superconsumer passion with great accuracy. For example, as explained earlier, the number of refrigerators and freezers a household owns is highly predictive of its willingness to buy an expensive standby power generator. If you own many refrigerators or freezers, then you store a lot of food that could go bad in a power outage. Under these circumstances, the ROI on buying an expensive standby generator is much higher. But as I showed earlier, it doesn't stop there. Having a standby generator is highly predictive of your willingness to buy more life insurance than you need, which is highly predictive of your willingness to be a superconsumer of vitamins. Find your most empathetic and best lateral thinkers—regardless of their day jobs—and they will help you accurately predict passion in other categories.

3. **Test and learn, refine and hone.** Once you have done steps 1 and 2, then it is a matter of putting it together and seeing how well it works via test-and-learn methods. It is important that you keep repeating the process; the world of big data and analytics is changing too rapidly to consider your prediction work a one-and-done effort. Companies need to regularly reevaluate the data-integration possibilities to build an ideal 360-degree view of consumers' passion. Pinpointing good forecasters of passion should be an evergreen effort and is often really fun, too. The goal is to keep reducing the amount of data you need to predict passion. The way you do it is by identifying the strongest leading indicators.

The world is migrating to individual data, but isn't quite there yet. More importantly, some companies go to market not at the individual level but at a higher level of aggregation (e.g., household, store, zip code, and region). It's more important that your data closely matches the level at which your company goes to market. If you are a direct-to-consumer business, then aim for individual-level data. If you go to market via retailers, then you don't need my exact address, but you need to know all the stores in a fifteen-mile radius that I might shop at. Most retailers can't change just one store, but they can change a cluster of stores in one local area.

The data could be shared with a wide array of people in the organization, not just the most important stakeholders. As I'll explain more in the last chapter, a superconsumer strategy, if executed well, should be accompanied by a change in culture. Everyone from the bottom up should know who your superconsumers are, why they love your products so much, and what motivates them.

If everyone in the organization, especially those who interact with consumers, are aware of the outsized impact that superconsumers have on your business, they'll be more willing to get behind the idea and spot superconsumers in the wild. It's also a good idea to humanize superconsumers as much as possible by sharing any tidbits and stories that you learned during interviews.

SHARING YOUR INSIGHTS WITHIN YOUR COMPANY

Your communication both with superconsumers and about them shouldn't be a onetime event. As superconsumers increasingly become a part of your business, you'll learn more and more about them as you would with anyone you have a relationship with. So keep talking about superconsumers and sharing information about them. And as other members of the team get to know your superconsumers in deeper ways, too, they'll be able to share new and valuable insights as well.

Next, you'll want to get together with functional experts in finance, sales, marketing, and the supply chain to make sure that everyone agrees on the profitability levers of your business at the gross-margin level (e.g., product profit and loss [P&L], brand P&L, and customer P&L) and the operating-margin level (e.g., fixed overhead, distribution density, and customer acquisition versus retention costs).

Instead of doing this through email, create a half-day work session. Have each functional area walk through the most important data for its most important decisions, and see if the spikes in profit overlap anywhere with the key data sets of each functional area. Hopefully, everyone will see the positive impact that superconsumers will have.

Once everyone is in agreement, you should establish the facts and principles that will guide everyone hereafter. These observations could be something like the following statements: These customers are more profitable to serve than others. These brands have higher margins.

These products run on the manufacturing lines that are underutilized and could use extra volume to cover factory overhead. These products utilize technology that we own rather than license. Increasing volume in these distribution routes would kill profitability.

I recommend creating a one-page summary of these facts and principles and making laminated copies. You could even attach the cards on lanyards so that people could wear them around their necks and carry with them into every meeting. It could be the most valuable half-day meeting you hold for your business.

Once you have done this with data on your own consumers, it is important to repeat these steps with the category's consumers. Often, your own consumer data and the category's consumer data are very similar. The trick here is defining your frame of reference. Let's say you make and sell beer. No doubt you compete with other beer brands of a similar type to yours. But you also probably compete with other beer styles and other alcoholic beverages like spirits and wine. So you need to find out more about superconsumers of those products as well. They may have much to say, and you may find much to learn.

By listening and engaging with superconsumers, sharing the information you learned with your team and others, and encouraging your colleagues to be more superconsumer-centric, you can help your organization become more and more aligned.

Throughout the process, there are three clear steps that help you focus your efforts:

1. Boil your superconsumer strategy down to as simple a statement as possible.

2. Write your goals and principles down, and have them close by so your team can refer to them.

3. Say them over and over again.

This process has worked well for Horst Schulze, the former CEO of the Ritz-Carlton Hotel Company and now of the Capella Hotel Group. Schulze has opened dozens of luxury hotels around the world—no easy task, considering the different markets and cultures he has had to navigate. One of the reasons for his success—and there are many—is his clarity: he knows exactly what *compass-correct* means for him, and he applies this approach to every aspect of his business. When he was a teenager, he worked in a luxury hotel near his hometown of Mosel, Germany. The hotel placed a priority on creating a great experience for guests, but it also shunned people like him. That experience led him to run his hotels in a different way. He wanted to create a luxury experience in which the staff was as important as the guests. His motto became "Ladies and gentlemen, serving ladies and gentlemen." I love the elegance and simplicity of that statement. It is incredibly hard to execute, but it is the north star for everything he does.[3]

Schulze has also come up with twenty-four ways to apply the statement to all areas of the hotel business. These ways are printed on pocket-sized laminated cards and given to employees. Before each shift, he has the staff read through some of the specific applications to make sure that every employee around the world is working toward the same goal.

Although Schulze's statement and its various applications aren't unique to superconsumers, they might as well be. His guests are looking for comfort and luxury, and he is empowering his staff to deliver those things. It's a virtuous circle.

For your own purposes, boiling down your strategy to a simple statement will take a lot of time and practice, as it should. Schulze, for example, created his statement after years and years of experience. It should be an iterative process.

So start now!

chapter 8

BUILDING A CULTURE

I know all too well that even the best strategies can be hard to implement, because of internal processes, misaligned incentives, and organizational structures that are difficult to navigate. And even if you're successful at overcoming those obstacles, it's very hard to keep up the momentum. Good leadership certainly helps, but more often than not, the organization will revert to business as usual. And superconsumer strategies are no exception: if you're not careful and diligent, your plan could sputter.

That's why it's imperative to ensure your strategy deeply resonates with your organizational culture.

With superconsumers, this is actually straightforward. And this is not just the superconsumers outside your organization who are passionate about your products and services. I'm talking about the superconsumers who are inside your organization, working at every level: the fashionista who works in the mail room at the headquarters of an apparel company, or the finance manager who works for a pork brand and who eats three pounds of bacon in any given week. My point is, inside the walls of your company, there are superconsumers who are passionate and engaged. So find them, ask questions, and let them help you. Let your superconsumers be superconsumers at work.

The key is to look beyond just the obvious places like marketing. Superconsumers can exist in your company across all functions. And they're sure to have great ideas about how to improve your products and business.

If there are superconsumers in your midst, and if they're encouraged to speak their minds, they will inject your culture with extra doses of energy, empathy, and creativity.

To give another example of finding superconsumers in your inner circle, I'll share one more story from my own life. I've shared many personal experiences and stories about my family in the book for one reason—and it's not because I have a secret wish to be a memoirist. It's because my personal life has shaped my ideas about superconsumers as much as my professional work has, and I'd encourage you to continue to comb your memories and relationships to learn more about consumer behavior, especially superconsumer behavior.

I have very personal and vivid food memories as a kid growing up in Hawaii. I remember my mother coming home after a long day at work and having to cook two dinners—a kid-friendly dinner for my brother and me and a traditional Korean dinner for my father and his parents. My mother had to put in double the work to make us all happy. I'm sure it was tough. But after I returned from a three-week trip to Korea with my church and had acquired a preference for Korean food, dinnertime became much easier and more fun for all of us.

Now as a dad of three kids, I have more empathy for my mom. I felt ashamed when my kids would look for macaroni and cheese on the menu when I took them to an Asian restaurant. I really wished my children and I could enjoy eating the same foods. So when Audrey, my middle child, began to enjoy Asian food, I was overjoyed. Because she was the swing vote in our family of five, her changing tastes opened up so many more food options for us.

Shared passion for the same foods may not seem like that big a deal, but it did unleash a lot of positivity. Audrey and I looked forward to our daddy-daughter dates, knowing that we would be eating something we both enjoyed. And our shared enthusiasm has spread to other members of the family as well. Since Audrey was competitive with her brother Luke, and vice versa, they would go out to eat and play the "who can try the most new foods?" game. Audrey and Miya (her older sister) found that we all love the Korean chicken wings at Great Seas in Chicago.

Our family now has more energy when we go out to eat, because besides thinking about what we want to order then, we're also thinking about what (and where) we'd like to eat in the future. There is more empathy. Now that the kids are more eager to try Asian food, I can relax a bit when they just want pizza. And there is more creativity. We tried to make chocolate soup dumplings at home (a failure). Food in our family is no longer a fight, but more fun.

This same trove of energy, empathy, and creativity can be found in the workplace. You need to unlock this source because although leadership is a critical part of executing a superconsumer strategy, you can't do it alone.

You need help. And the more people at your disposal who understand the unique characteristics and motivations of superconsumers, the more likely you are to succeed.

Let's look at some insights from other leaders who have implemented superconsumer strategies and who can speak to the benefits of having superconsumers throughout the organization.

UNLOCKING ENERGY

The airline industry has experienced great volatility from deregulation, takeovers through mergers and acquisitions, and, as always, unpredictable forces of nature. So when I asked Mark Krolick—managing director of marketing and product development at United Airlines—about the hypothesis that having more superconsumers as leaders or employees enhances business performance, he smiled. "My guess is that one hundred percent of United's employees are superconsumers of travel," he said. "The romance of travel is near and dear to everyone's heart. There can be a lot of stress in this industry. It's not for everyone. But our employees know this full well and embrace this because it is a labor of love."

Krolick also noted that a meaningful number of United Airlines employees are also pilots—these are super-superconsumers. Krolick himself is a pilot, and although he does admit that his pilot skills don't necessarily help him out in the day-to-day aspects of marketing, they do help him appreciate the challenges that exist on the front lines and cross-functionally. "The learning curve in any industry is steep, but it is particularly so in the airline industry. The superconsumer effect is realized in more loyalty, lower turnover for United and in the industry. Longer tenure reduces the challenge of a steep learning curve."

Krolick made another critical point. Having lots of superconsumers at United Airlines made it easier to compete for talent among millennials, who tend to pursue their passions more so than do other generations, as passionate people are inclined to flock toward other passionate people.

Keith Levy, who oversaw the creation of Bud Light Lime and other similar products as vice president of marketing and sales for Anheuser-Busch, took a similar stand on in-house superconsumers. He estimated that 95 percent of Anheuser-Busch employees loved and enjoyed beer and the remaining 5 percent loved beer but could not drink it for medical reasons like celiac disease. The passion was infectious. Levy told me that his wife would accost people for drinking a competitor's beer. Levy, now at Royal Canin, a pet food company, told me that the same employee passion holds true there. Once his employees start feeding their pets Royal Canin and seeing the clear benefits, they become much more energized and work harder because they have firsthand experience of the impact of the products they are making and selling.

Both Krolick and Levy highlight a seminal point: passion is not a finite resource. Time is a finite resource, but energy is not. In one of my favorite *Harvard Business Review* articles, "Manage Your Energy, Not Your Time," Tony Schwartz and Catherine McCarthy go deeper into energy: "Defined in physics as the capacity to work, energy comes from four main wellsprings in human beings: the body, emotions, mind, and spirit. In each, energy can be systematically expanded and regularly renewed."[1] Energy is an expanded resource that few companies fully tap into. Schwartz and McCarthy describe how to access this energy: "To effectively reenergize their workforces, organizations need to shift their emphasis from getting more out of people to investing more in them, so they are motivated—and able—to bring more of themselves to work every day." Sounds like letting superconsumers be superconsumers at work, doesn't it? The authors tested the idea of renewing a workforce's energy at Wachovia Bank (now Wells Fargo). They found that a group whose energy had been renewed and otherwise supported generated 13 percent higher revenues from loans and 20 percent higher revenues from deposits in one year than did a group without this support.

BUILDING EMPATHY

I spoke with Patty McCord, the former chief talent officer of Netflix from 1998 to 2013. During her tenure, Netflix stock grew more than forty times bigger, so she speaks with authority about building a high-performance company. In fact, she literally wrote the book on it. Along with Reed Hastings, Netflix's founder and CEO, she wrote a PowerPoint presentation on Netflix culture. The presentation quickly went viral and has been viewed more than five million times. Sheryl Sandberg, chief operations officer of Facebook, called McCord and Hasting's presentation the most important document ever to come out of Silicon Valley.[2]

Since Netflix employees were binge-watchers in their personal lives, they were empathetic to the viewing habits and behaviors of their consumers, especially when Netflix went from DVD-by-mail to streaming. Because employees themselves tended to hide their guilty pleasures—the TV shows and movies they liked but which they'd never admit to others—they saw an opportunity: "When streaming came," McCord said, "all of us working at Netflix realized that it opened up a new category of movies and TV shows. This was 'junk food' TV and movies that we all secretly enjoyed watching, but didn't necessarily want it publicly displayed on our desks. We often had fun kidding each other about that."

And as they could more precisely measure consumer behavior—what people were watching, when they joined, when they watched, if their streaming behavior was increasing or decreasing—employees could parse the information more meaningfully because they truly understood and emphasized with their consumers rather than treating them like data points. "It was as if our consumers were sitting right next to me at the company," McCord said. "And guess what—we discovered we were no different than our consumers . . . We stopped judging our consumers and ourselves about our media habits.

And that freed us to better serve our consumers because we understood their needs without judging them."

As media enthusiasts themselves, Netflix's employees were self-aware enough to realize that consumers have a variety of tastes and that there was no reason to stick exclusively to proud-to-watch content. And self-awareness, according to McCord, is ultimately the key to Netflix's success because it "makes it so much easier to put the customer first. Self-awareness makes it easier to be selfless."

INSPIRING CREATIVITY

More often than not, we look for creativity from senior executives and so-called high-potential employees. These employees are very important, of course, but as Michelle Stacy, the former president of Keurig, and Man Jit Singh, the president of Sony Home Entertainment Pictures, told me, there are two groups of employees that we often overlook: those in the middle of the organization and younger employees, or millennials.

Stacy has the distinction of leading large organizations like Oral-B at Gillette and small but fast-growing organizations like Keurig, where she presided as president from 2008 to 2014. By managing through Keurig's rapid growth—from $1 billion in revenue to over $4 billion during her tenure—she fully realized the power of the middle.

"As leaders," she said, "it is always so easy for us to lean toward the stars in an organization. We can count on them. They are usually more highly motivated and need less direction so we gravitate toward them and choose to spend our time with them. However, it's the middle of the organization that needs our time. They will benefit the most from being mentored. They need to feel valuable and that they are being developed. When this middle feels valued, then they stay engaged."

Since Keurig was growing at a fast clip, Stacy knew that she needed to create a culture full of employees who loved coffee as much as their consumers did and who were dedicated to the company: "We couldn't get paralyzed. We had to reward risk taking and initiatives. And that is where the middle was invaluable. We were growing so fast it was hard to oversee everything. That our employees loved a wide variety of coffee . . . like our consumers [did] made it easier to trust they would do the right thing." Being in the lobby of Keurig and seeing the sea of coffee choices is like being a kid in a candy store if you love coffee. The sense of adventure, exploration, and discovery when you first walk into the building is a daily reminder of the joyful experience Keurig is trying to provide to each consumer.

Like Stacy, Singh knows the hidden value of overlooked employees. As a young man at the beginning of his career, he sold instant noodles in India, and even though it was a crowded and competitive space, he was very successful. Singh attributes a good part of his success to his own love for instant noodles and the brand he was selling, which made him work harder. Because of his experience, he knows the impact that younger employees can have on an organization if they are properly motivated.

This is why he often taps into the millennials at Sony to drive better business results, he said: "Millennials have so many more options for employment, from big companies to up-and-coming companies to their own startups. Passion for movies is part of how Sony can attract and keep top talent. But millennials are also critical to keep up with change, because more has changed in the last two years than the prior twenty years of movies."

Take the movie *The 5th Wave*, for example. Based on a best-selling young-adult novel by Rick Yancey about a sixteen-year-old girl who is one of the few survivors of an alien attack, the movie wasn't exactly in the wheelhouse of Sony execs, who were much older than the potential audience. So Singh found younger Sony employees who were familiar with the content and were able to offer opinions and insights into the main character, played by Chloe Moretz. These employees' input meaningfully changed how Sony marketed the movie. With their help, the sci-fi movie grossed over $110 million at the box office, which is nearly triple its operating budget of $38 million. The young Sony contingent also helped the higher-ups create a unique DVD bundle with premium foil packaging and extra video content from the red-carpet premiere that would appeal to the film's audience. "When you ride the elevator with a Sony Home Entertainment Pictures employee, ask them about superconsumers," Singh said. "They will know exactly what you're talking about, no matter how junior they are, or what role they have. We have embedded superconsumers into our culture very deeply."

Most leaders recognize that culture is critical, but sometimes it is hard to quantify the benefits. But unleashing a culture of superconsumers has clear benefits. Let's say that the increased energy from a superconsumer culture produces 10 percent more labor productivity. People go the extra mile and may be willing to stay a little late because it is fun. Would you rather drive productivity that way or increase your labor costs by 10 percent? If this example sounds like a fantasy, consider Gallup's observation that only 32.5 percent of US employees are engaged at work.[3] According to this pollster, 50.8 percent of employees are "not engaged," and 17.2 percent are "actively disengaged." You probably can't do much about the 17.2 percent who are actively disengaged—who alone cost the United States $450 billion to $550 billion in lost productivity, according to Gallup. But most likely, a reasonable number of the middle 50 percent are themselves superconsumers or have a close family or friend who is a superconsumer of the category they work in. Couldn't you reach them this way?

Let's say that the empathy in your company increases 10 percent because of a superconsumer culture. Certainly, this increase will clearly benefit your external metrics like customer satisfaction scores. But empathy has internal benefits, too. By flattening a hierarchical structure, empathy can empower all the workforce and, ultimately, your organization. Consider Nordstrom's purpose: "To provide a fabulous customer experience by empowering customers and their employees who serve them." Not only has this purpose served Nordstrom well for decades, but it has helped the company overcome the multichannel challenges most retailers struggle with. One of the biggest obstacles for brick-and-mortar retailers that are trying to win online as well is internal organizational conflict. If a customer is in the store, but buys it on a phone online, who gets the sale—the physical store or the e-commerce site? Nordstrom has increased its sales by 50 percent from 2010 to 2015 through both online and offline sales.[4] It achieved this growth by arming its store employees with digital information about their shoppers' past purchases and enabling mobile checkout without the need to send the shopper to a cash register. The retailer also has an app that alerts employees to the latest trends on Pinterest. All of this digital technology—be it apps, analytics, or social media tools—is tightly integrated to serve the customer via Nordstrom's empowered employees.

As the final benefit of a superconsumer culture, creativity has perhaps the greatest upside but the widest variability. A great example of creativity from superconsumers in your midst is what happened to Steve Hughes, the CEO of Sunrise Strategic Partners (a $300 million private equity fund). Hughes was inspired to create Grovestand brand orange juice when he was working for Tropicana and paid attention to some superconsumers right under his nose. While walking the factory lines one day, he noticed some plant workers on break. They were drinking orange juice and adding back to their drinks the pulp that the machines had separated from the juice. Curious, Hughes asked them why they were doing this. They told him that the pulp made the juice seem as if it were freshly squeezed. Creativity from superconsumers from within provided the creative spark that launched a huge innovation.

In the end, the incremental value of a superconsumer culture may in fact exceed the value of any superconsumer strategy. A shift in consumers, increased competition, or some unexpected external shock may require a tweak in strategy over the years. But a strong superconsumer culture, where the newest entry-level employee can offer an opinion on growth because he or she is a superconsumer, has an impact that can last decades. A strong superconsumer culture, where employees are willing to give a bit more because they know what their customers are feeling, can be the difference maker in a hypercompetitive world.

Is there any one of us who doesn't wish that our workplace had more energy, empathy, and creativity? Who wouldn't want to work at a place like that?

notes

Chapter 1

1. KPMG International, *Forecasting with Confidence*, publication 308-743, September 2007, http://www.kpmg.com/dutchcaribbean/en/services/Advisory/Documents/forecasting-with-confidence.pdf.

2. Larry Kim, "30 Inspiring Billion-Dollar Startup Company Mission Statements," *Inc.*, November 5, 2015.

Chapter 3

1. Tuck Communications, "Private-Label Products in the Manufacturer-Retailer Power Balance," *Tuck Today* (Tuck School of Business at Dartmouth), Fall 2008 (published online on August 19, 2010, http://www.tuck.dartmouth.edu/news/articles/private-label-products-in-the-manufacturer-retailer-power-balance).

2. Karen Collier and Chad Van Estrop, "Time Supermarket Customers Spend at Different Shelves Is Revealed," *(Victoria) Herald Sun*, August 30, 2014, http://www.heraldsun.com.au/news/victoria/time-supermarket-customers-spend-at-different-shelves-is-revealed/news-story/73d4c3d5f7d79ac75325394fedfe64ad?nk=f716a343a39cb7c3b3df446d7d4e8c48-1466561013.

3. Nielsen, *The U.S. Breakthrough Innovation Report 2016*, June 27, 2016, http://www.nielsen.com/us/en/solutions-new/capabilities/breakthrough-innovation.html.

Chapter 4

1. Michael Maoz, "How American Girl Can Teach Your CEO About Social Media," *Gartner Blog Network*, January 18, 2011; Mark Lino, *Expenditures on Children by Families*, no. 1528-2013 (Washington, DC: US Department of Agriculture, Center for Nutrition Policy and Promotion, 2013).

2. Eddie Yoon and Linda Deeken, "Why It Pays to Be a Category Creator," *Harvard Business Review*, March 2013, https://hbr.org/2013/03/why-it-pays-to-be-a-category-creator.

3. Malcom Gladwell, *The Tipping Point: How Little Things Can Make a Difference* (Boston: Little, Brown, 2000), 132, 173, and back cover.

4. Nielsen, Superconsumer Salon Session, 2014.

5. Data from the Cambridge Group, 2014.

6. Kurt Soller, "Bear Market, How the Griz Coat Became a Millennial Phenomenon," *Bloomberg*, October 23, 2014, http://www.bloomberg.com/news/articles/2014-10-23/griz-coat-bear-costume-becomes-millennial-phenomenon.

7. "$100 Million Pledged to Independent Film," *The Kickstarter Blog*, January 3, 2014, https://www.kickstarter.com/blog/100-million-pledged-to-independent-film; and Kickstarter, "Stats," https://www.kickstarter.com/help/stats.

8. Al Ramadan, "Behind Uber's Soaring Value," *Fortune,* December 11, 2014, http://fortune.com/author/christopher-lochhead.

9. Al Ramadan, Christopher Lochhead, Dave Peterson, and Kevin Maney, "Time to Market Cap: The New Metric That Matters," Play Bigger, LLC, https://playbigger.com/files/PlayBiggerTTMCReport.pdf.

10. Scott Berinato, "Reusable Bags Make People Buy Organic—and Junk: An Interview with Uma Karmarkar," *Harvard Business Review*, April 2015, https://hbr.org/2015/04/reusable-bags-make-people-buy-organicand-junk.

11. Rob Wengel and Taddy Hall, "How to Flip 85% Misses to 85% Hits: Lessons from the Nielsen Breakthrough Innovation

Project," Nielsen, June 24, 2014, http://www.nielsen.com/us/en/insights/news/2014/how-to-flip-85-misses-to85-hits-lessons-from-the-nielsen-breakthrough-innovation-project.html.

Chapter 5

1. Sheryl Sandberg, *Lean In: Women, Work, and the Will to Lead* (New York: Alfred A. Knopf, 2013).

2. CNBC, "Top 20 Beer Drinking Countries," CNBC graphic, accessed June 25, 2016, http://www.cnbc.com/2008/09/22/Top-20-Beer-Drinking-Countries.html.

3. MarketWatch, "Ten States Where People Drink the Most Beer," *MarketWatch*, July 28, 2015, www.marketwatch.com/story/10-states-where-people-drink-the-most-beer-2015-07-07?page=1.

4. *Church of the Customer Blog*, "The 1% Rule: Charting Citizen Participation," May 5, 2006, http://web.archive.org/web/20100511081141/http://www.churchofthecustomer.com/blog/2006/05/charting_wiki_p.html.

5. Heather Long, "Twenty-Three Percent of American Homes Have Two Fridges," CNN Money, May 27, 2016, http://money.cnn.com/2016/05/27/news/economy/23-percent-of-american-homes-have-2-fridges/; and Bill McNary and Chip Berry, "How Americans Are Using Energy in Homes Today," American Council for an Energy-Efficient Economy, 2012, http://aceee.org/files/proceedings/2012/data/papers/0193-000024.pdf.

6. Jason Notte, "These 11 Brewers Make Over 90% of All U.S. Beer," *MarketWatch*, July 28, 2015, http://www.marketwatch.com/story/these-11-brewers-make-over-90-of-all-us-beer-2015-07-27.

7. For components of Starbucks products, see "What the Starbucks?!" infographic, Alternet.org, accessed June 15, 2016, http://www.alternet.org/files/story_images/gmo-inside-starbucks-crop-to-crop-infographic-11x7.jpg.

8. This section is adapted from Eddie Yoon, "The Generosity Strategies That Help Companies Grow," *Harvard Business Review*, May 2, 2013, https://hbr.org/2013/05/netflix-reported-another-great.

9. Kenneth Hein, "In-Store Sampling Boosts Repeat Purchases," *Adweek*, August 4, 2009, http://www.adweek.com/news/advertising-branding/store-sampling-boosts-repeat-pur-chases-106208; and "Groundbreaking Study Redefines In-Store Sampling Impact and Usage," Businesswire, August 3, 2009, http://www.businesswire.com/news/home/20090803005049/en/Groundbreaking-Study-Redefines-In-Store-Sampling-Impact-Usage.

10. "Binge Viewing," ThinkTV.com, June 4, 2014, http://www.tvb.ca/pages/Binge_viewing.

11. Rip Empson, "Netflix Says Fewer Than 8,000 People 'Gamed' Its Free Trials to Watch *House of Cards*," Techcrunch.com, April 22, 2013, https://techcrunch.com/2013/04/22/netflix-says-less-than-8000-people-gamed-its-free-trials-to-watch-house-of-cards/.

12. Netflix, Inc., Form 8-K, Securities and Exchange Commission, April 22, 2013, https://ir.netflix.com/secfiling.cfm?filingID=1065280-13-11&CIK=1065280; Craig Smith, "By the Numbers: 80 Amazing Netflix Statistics and Facts," DMR, July 31, 2016, http://expandedramblings.com/index.php/netflix_statistics-facts/; and David Hinckley, "Americans Spend 34 Hours a Week Watching TV, According to Nielsen Numbers," *New York Daily News*, September 19, 2012, http://www.nydailynews.com/entertainment/tv-movies/americans-spend-34-hours-week-watching-tv-nielsen-numbers-article-1.1162285

13. Martha C. White, "At Panera's Pay-What-You-Want Cafés, Customers Usually Pay Full Price," *Time*, February 27, 2012, http://business.time.com/2012/02/27/at-paneras-pay-what-you-want-cafes-customers-usually-pay-full-price/.

14. James B. Stewart, "Netflix Looks Back on Its Near-Death Spiral," *New York Times*, April 26, 2013.

Chapter 6

1. "Online Gaming and Digital Distribution," Parks Associates, 2011, https://www.parksassociates.com/services/onlinegaming.

2. *Global Games Market Report*, Newzoo, 2016, https://newzoo.com/solutions/revenues-projections/global-games-market-report/.

3. Austin Carr, "The Messy Business of Re-inventing Happiness," *Fast Company*, April 15, 2015, http://www.fastcompany.com/3044283/the-messy-business-of-reinventing-happiness.

4. Chris Foswick and Don Johnson, "MBPT Spotlight: The Secret of Empire's Success: Fox's Mid-Season Gamble Shows That Culturally Relevant Programming Can Drive Mass Appeal," Broadcasting Cable, September 25, 2015, http://www.broadcastingcable.com/news/currency/mbpt-spotlight-secret-empires-success-foxs-mid-season-gamble-shows-culturally-relevant-programming-can-drive-mass-appeal/144494.

5. "Swrve Finds 0.15% of Mobile Gamers Contribute 50% of all In-Game Revenue," Swrve, February 26, 2014, https://www.swrve.com/company/press/swrve-finds-015-of-mobile-gamers-contribute-50-of-all-in-game-revenue.

6. DataGenetics, "Facebook Casual Game Demographics," http://www.datagenetics.com/blog/december12010/.

Chapter 7

1. Nielsen, *U.S. Breakthrough Innovation Report 2016*, June 27, 2016, http://www.nielsen.com/us/en/insights/reports/2016/the-us-breakthrough-innovation-report-2016.html.

2. Meaghan O'Connell, "Thank God We Live in the Era of the Fashion Rash Guard," *New York Magazine*, April 21, 2016, http://nymag.com/thecut/2016/04/thank-god-for-the-fashion-rash-guard.html. Emphasis in original.

3. "Horst Schulze Operates the World's Best Hotels," Hospitalitynet.org, April 20, 2012, http://www.hospitalitynet.org/news/4055772.html; and "GLS15 Horst Schulze: Creating World Class Service," Global Leadership Summit, August 7, 2015, http://www.followthegls.com/uncategorized/gls15-horst-schulze-creating-world-class-service/.

Chapter 8

1. Tony Schwartz and Catherine McCarthy, "Manage Your Energy, Not Your Time," *Harvard Business Review*, October 2007, https://hbr.org/2007/10/manage-your-energy-not-your-time.

2. For Sandberg statement and the PowerPoint presentation, see Patty McCord, "How Netflix Reinvented HR," *Harvard Business Review*, January–February 2014, https://hbr.org/2014/01/how-netflix-reinvented-hr.

3. Gallup Employee Engagement, January 13, 2016.

4. Jeanne Ross, Cynthia M. Beath, and Ina Sebastian, "Why Nordstrom's Digital Strategy Works (and Yours Probably Doesn't)," *Harvard Business Review*, January 14, 2015, https://hbr.org/2015/01/why-nordstroms-digital-strategy-works-and-yours-probably-doesnt.

index

acknowledgments

To borrow a phrase from J. R. R. Tolkien, this book was an unexpected journey. Being an author was not a path I foresaw for myself, nor was it something I was trained for. For most of my life I considered myself more of a numbers guy than someone adept with words. Early in my professional career I advanced more on the strength of my analytic and mathematic skills than I did on my skill as a writer.

I love music, and music is essentially math—megahertz, decibels, and rhythm—mixed with storytelling (lyrics, backstory, and soul). Music has power because stories have power.

Part of the joy of working at The Cambridge Group is how easily and regularly stories emerge from behind the numbers, thanks to the "lyrics" supplied by consumers. So much of consulting is just numbers without soul and, inversely, most consumer work is just emotion without numbers—no music there. At The Cambridge Group, stories fall off the bone of every project, much the way tender morsels fall off perfectly cooked ribs.

My nearly two decades at The Cambridge Group have been a storytelling feast. Each year yielded more stories—an unusual set of numbers that came to life via super-consumer lyrics, performed by clients to drive billions of dollars of profitable growth. The more stories I collected, the better storyteller I became. And the better storyteller I became, the easier it was to write.

And for that I have a number of people to thank.

I have my dad to thank for my love of music and my mom to thank for my love of math. Even more important, I thank my parents for sacrificing their stories in Korea and starting over in America, where they could build a better story for my brother and me. Thanks to Jimmy for being a fun, patient brother and super uncle. 감사합니다

Thanks to my in-laws: Dr. Joseph and Pauline Oyama, Dr. Mark and Lori Oyama and their son Oliver, Joel and Jen Murphy and their daughters Kaitlin and Emily, my brother's wife Doris and their two girls, Ella and Jackie. Thank you for sharing your stories and for your love and support over the years.

Thanks also to Rick Kash, founder of The Cambridge Group, and to all my Cambridge mentors, including

Kevin Bowen, Peter Klein, Bruce Onsager, Laura Farwell, Michal Clements, Gloria Cox, Navtej Nandra, and Steve Carlotti. Thanks to all my fellow Principals who have helped make The Cambridge Group a special place: Jim Eckels, Chris Fosdick, Taddy Hall, Don Johnson, Tim Joyce, Pete Killian, and Ellen Turner. And thank you to TCGers Dimitar Antov, Jeremy Bartlow, Lindsey Leikhim, Amanda Budow, and Claire Zhou, whose contributions made this a better book.

Special thanks to Jason Green for his longtime friendship, leadership by example, and unique blend of humor and humility, insight and integrity. Special thanks to Mark Henneman, my thought leadership buddy who was always willing to indulge me in fun "what if" flights of fancy mixed with gentle reminders of reality. Special thanks to Linda Deeken, TCG's director of marketing, who was there with me when I first started writing and generously invested so much of her heart, soul, and supersmarts into building our thought leadership team while raising five children.

Thanks to our Nielsen friends and key leaders: Dave Calhoun, Mitch Barns, John Lewis, and Mark Leiter, and to all my GLP 2010 team, who welcomed us and made a home for The Cambridge Group. Thanks as well to Jeff

Eastman and his team for all their help with data and analytics, and also to Courtney Ramirez and Tom Duffy for helping us get the word out.

I am grateful to the wonderful team at *Harvard Business Review*, who have been amazing to work with over the years. Thanks to Tim Sullivan, Sarah McConville, Kevin Evers, Jen Waring, and Nina Nocciolino. Special thanks to Dan McGinn, who has been my editor and friend for the last five years and who patiently and persistently made me a better writer and thinker. Together, you are an embarrassment of riches.

I owe much to my clients and business leaders, from whom I have learned so much and been blessed to partner with over the years: Jeff Ackerberg, Mukul Deoras, Steve Clapp, Carl Gerlach, Tim Zimmer, Steve Hughes, Keith Levy, Marlene Coulis, Michelle Stacy, Dwight Brown, Greg Gallagher, Dave Behringer, Nigel Kirtley, George Zoghbi, Michael Fox, Jess Aguirre, and so many others. Thanks to Man Jit Singh, Patty McCord, and Mark Krolick for your thinking and contributions to the book. It has been a joy and an honor to watch you lead. Mahalo!

Thanks also to my longtime friends Hugh Kim, Sam Park, Emmett Tomai, and Reid Townsend for walking with me through life and for encouraging me in this process. The older I get, the more grateful I am for your enduring friendship.

Thanks to my children, not only for the fun and joy you bring to my life, but for all you have taught me. Luke, I love your nonstop imagination and the power of your perseverance. Audrey, your secret poems and your loving-kindness provide endless joy. Miya, I can't decide if I'm more impressed with the beauty of your Chibi drawings or the fact that you taught yourself how to create them.

Finally, thank you to my wife Kristen. Bread and butter are we. Thank you for the sacrifices you made while I was writing this book. Thank you for putting your career on hold to allow me to have fun in mine. And most of all, thank you for caring enough to critique my work. I've enjoyed tremendously our research project thus far. I can't wait to see the next chapters unfold and how they connect with the ultimate story.

about the author

Eddie Yoon is a Principal with The Cambridge Group, a growth-strategy firm that is part of Nielsen. Over his seventeen years at TCG, he has helped clients drive over $1 billion of profitable growth in the areas of consumer packaged goods, retail, media, and technology. He is an expert in superconsumers, category creation, marketing, innovation, and retail execution.

Yoon earned his BA from the University of Chicago, in Political Science and Economics. He has researched, written, and spoken on the topics of growth strategy, superconsumers, category creation, and latent demand. He has written dozens of articles for hbr.org and been quoted in the *Wall Street Journal*. He has spoken on these topics at conferences in the United States, Asia, Australia, and New Zealand.

Yoon lives with his wife Kristen and their three children in the suburbs of Chicago. He was born and raised in Hawaii and returns there as often as he can.